The Brave New World of Work

The Brave New World of Work

Ulrich Beck

Translated by Patrick Camiller

Polity Press

This translation © Polity Press 2000. First published in German as
Schöne neue Arbeitswelt. Vision Weltbürgergesellschaft, © Campus Verlag,
Frankfurt/New York, 1999.

First published in 2000 by Polity Press in association with Blackwell
Publishers Ltd

Reprinted 2000

Published with the assistance of Inter Nationes, Bonn

Editorial office:
Polity Press
65 Bridge Street
Cambridge CB2 1UR, UK

Published in the USA by
Blackwell Publishers Inc.
350 Main Street
Malden, MA 02148, USA

Marketing and production:
Blackwell Publishers Ltd
108 Cowley Road
Oxford OX4 1JF, UK

A catalogue record for this book is available from the British Library.

Library of Congress Cataloging-in-Publication Data

Beck, Ulrich, 1944–
    [Schöne neue Arbeitswelt. English]
    The brave new world of work / Ulrich Beck ; translated by Patrick Camiller.
      p. cm.
    Includes bibliographical references and index.
    ISBN 0-7456-2397-2 — ISBN 0-7456-2398-0
      1. Labor — Social aspects. 2. Work — Social aspects. I. Title.
  HD4901 .B393 2000
  306.3'6 — dc21
                                            99-058486

Typeset in 11 on 13pt Berling
by Best-set Typesetter Ltd., Hong Kong
Printed in Great Britain by MPG Books, Bodmin, Cornwall

This book is printed on acid-free paper.

Contents

1

The Brazilianization of the West

Two Scenarios, One Introduction

The unintended consequence of the neoliberal free-market utopia is a Brazilianization of the West. For trends already visible in world society – high unemployment in the countries of Europe, the so-called jobs miracle in the United States, the transition from a work society to a knowledge society – do not involve a change only in the content of work. Equally remarkable is the new similarity in how paid work itself is shaping up in the so-called first world and the so-called third world; the spread of temporary and insecure employment, discontinuity and loose informality into Western societies that have hitherto been the bastions of full employment. The social structure in the heartlands of the West is thus coming to resemble the patchwork quilt of the South, characterized by diversity, unclarity and insecurity in people's work and life.

The political economy of insecurity

In a semi-industrialized country such as Brazil, those who depend upon a wage or salary in full-time work represent only a minority of the economically active population; the majority earn their living in more precarious conditions. People are travelling vendors, small retailers or craftworkers, offer all kinds of personal service, or shuttle back and forth between different fields of activity, forms

1

of employment and training. As new developments show in the so-called highly developed economies, this nomadic 'multi-activity' – until now mainly a feature of female labour in the West – is not a premodern relic but a rapidly spreading variant in the late work-societies, where attractive, highly skilled and well-paid full-time employment is on its way out.

Trends in Germany may stand here for those in other Western societies. In the 1960s only a tenth of employees belonged to this precarious group; by the 1970s the figure had risen to a quarter, and in the late 1990s it is a third. If change continues at this speed – and there is much to suggest that it will – in another ten years only a half of employees will hold a full-time job for a long period of their lives, and the other half will, so to speak, work *à la brésilienne*.

Here we can see the outlines of what a political economy of insecurity, or a political economy of world risk society, needs to analyse and theorize in greater detail.

1 In the political economy of insecurity, the new power game and the new power differential are acted out between territorially fixed political players (governments, parliaments, trade unions) and non-territorially fixed economic players (capital, finance and commerce).

2 This creates a well-founded impression that the room for manoeuvre of individual states is limited to the following dilemma: either pay with higher unemployment for levels of poverty that do no more than steadily increase (as in most European countries), or accept spectacular poverty in exchange for a little less unemployment (as in the United States).

3 This is bound up with the fact that the work society is coming to an end, as more and more people are ousted by smart technologies. 'To our counterparts at the end of the 21st century today's struggles over jobs will seem like a fight over deckchairs on the *Titanic*.'[1] The 'job for life' has disappeared. Thus, rising unemployment can no longer be explained in terms of cyclical economic crises; it is due rather to the successes of technologically advanced capitalism. The old arsenal of economic policies cannot deliver results, and all paid work is subject to the threat of replacement.

4 The political economy of insecurity therefore has to deal with a domino effect. Those factors which in good times used to complement and reinforce one another – full employment, guaran-

2

teed pensions, high tax revenue, leeway in public policy – are now facing knock-on dangers. Paid employment is becoming precarious; the foundations of the social-welfare state are collapsing; normal life-stories are breaking up into fragments; old age poverty is programmed in advance; and the growing demands on welfare protection cannot be met from the empty coffers of local authorities.

5 'Labour market flexibility' has become a political mantra. The orthodox defensive strategies, then, are themselves thrown onto the defensive. Calls are made everywhere for greater 'flexibility' – or, in other words, that employers should be able to fire employees with less difficulty. Flexibility also means a redistribution of risks away from the state and the economy towards the individual. The jobs on offer become short-term and easily terminable (i.e. 'renewable'). And finally, flexibility means: 'Cheer up, your skills and knowledge are obsolete, and no one can say what you must learn in order to be needed in the future.'

The upshot is that the more work relations are 'deregulated' and 'flexibilized', the faster work society changes into a risk society incalculable both in terms of individual lives and at the level of the state and politics, and the more important it becomes to grasp the political economy of risk in its contradictory consequences for economics, politics and society.[2] Anyway, one future trend is clear. For a majority of people, even in the apparently prosperous middle layers, their basic existence and lifeworld will be marked by endemic insecurity. More and more individuals are encouraged to perform as a 'Me & Co.', selling themselves on the marketplace.

The picture of society thus changes dramatically under the influence of a political economy of insecurity. Extremes of clarity appear in small zones at the very top as well as the very bottom, so low down that it is no longer really a bottom but an outside. But in between, ambivalence is the rule in a welter of jumbled forms. More and more people today live, so to speak, between the categories of poor and rich.

It is quite possible, however, to define or reconstruct these inter-categorial existences within a 'social structure of ambivalence'. To this extent, we may therefore speak of a clear-cut ambivalence. In contrast to class society, divided between proletariat and bourgeoisie, the political economy of ambivalence produces not a

Neither-Nor but a Both-And culture. This means, first of all, that top and bottom are no longer clearly defined poles, but overlap and fuse in new ways into a kind of wealth-aspect/poverty-aspect or into fixed-term wealth with its corresponding forms of existence. Consequently, insecurity prevails in nearly all positions within society. In accordance with relative weight in knowledge and capital, this leads to splits in societies and perhaps even to the collective decline of whole groups of countries. At first this may be symbolically covered over – discursively 'sweetened', as it were – by the rhetoric of 'independent entrepreneurial individualism'. But it cannot be concealed for long that the bases of the much-praised welfare state and a lively everyday democracy, together with the whole self-image of a worker-citizen society based on 'institutionalized class compromise', are falling apart.[3]

The euro currency experiment is thus beginning at a time when, with the irrevocable loss of full employment in the classical sense, Europe's postwar project and its understanding of itself are in a state of suspense. As global capitalism, in the countries of the West, dissolves the core values of the work society, a historical bond is broken between capitalism, welfare state and democracy. Let there be no mistake. A property-owning capitalism that aims at nothing other than profit, excluding from consideration employees, welfare state and democracy, is a capitalism that surrenders its own legitimacy. The neoliberal utopia is a kind of democratic illiteracy. For the market is not its own justification; it is an economic form viable only in interplay with material security, social rights and democracy, and hence with the democratic state. To gamble everything on the free market is to destroy, along with democracy, that whole economic mode. The turmoil on the international finance markets of Asia, Russia and South America in the autumn of 1998 gives only a foretaste of what lies down that road.

No one today questions capitalism. Who indeed would risk doing so? The only powerful opponent of capitalism is profit-only capitalism itself. Bad news on the labour market counts as a victory report on Wall Street, the simple calculation being that profits rise when labour costs fall.

What robs technologically advanced capitalism of its legitimacy is not that it tears down national barriers and produces ever more with ever less labour, but rather that it blocks political initiatives towards a new European social model and social contract. Anyone

4

today who thinks about unemployment should not remain trapped in old disputes about the 'second labour market', 'falling wage costs' or 'affirmative action'. The question that needs to be asked is how democracy will be possible after the full-employment society. What appears as a final collapse must instead be converted into a founding period for new ideas and models, a period that will open the way to the state, economy and society of the twenty-first century.

The right to breaks in lifetime economic activity

The 'pessimistic optimist' André Gorz argues that if no recipes are useful any more, the only option is to recognize the 'crisis' and to make it the basis of a new normality. 'We are leaving behind the work society, without seeking the outlines of a new society,' writes Gorz. And in the poverty of the present, he detects the outlines of an alternative way forward for society, which matches up anew security and liberty for all. 'We know, feel and grasp that we are all potentially unemployed or underemployed, part-time or makeshift workers without any real job security. But what each of us knows individually has not yet become an awareness of our new common reality.' Only after the oath of manifestation – which reads: 'The free market utopia is not the solution but a major cause of the problem, and even new turbo-growth will not revive the good old full-employment society' – is it possible to delineate a new social model and the paths towards it. André Gorz sketches out a change of perspective whereby lack of work becomes an abundance of time, and low growth an impetus to become self-active.[4]

I propose to go one crucial step further. The antithesis to the work society is a strengthening of the political society of individuals, of active civil society here and now, of a civil democracy in Europe that is at once local and transnational. This society of active citizens, which is no longer fixed within the container of the national state and whose activities are organized both locally and across frontiers, can find and develop answers to the challenges of the second modernity – namely, individualization, globalization, falling employment and ecological crisis. For in this way communal demoracy and identity are given new life in projects such as ecological initiatives, Agenda 21, work with homeless people, local theatres, cultural centres and meeting-places for discussion.

In place of a society fixated on paid work, this vision offers the prospect of gradually gaining sovereignty over time and experiencing political freedom within self-organized activity networks. Nevertheless, it raises a number of thorny questions, which will be addressed later, in Chapters 8 and 9. To name but two: How can spontaneity be organized? Is all this not just an ideology which frees the state, especially the welfare state, from the responsibilities of public provision?

Civil society and direct democracy presuppose that citizens are able to find the energy for active involvement. But does this not exclude those who cannot participate in social and political life because they are under intense economic pressure or actually on the brink of ruin? Does the idea of a citizens' democracy not derive from a middle-class idyll? And will it not be actually counter-productive, by creating a cheap-wage sector that thins down regular paid labour?

Furthermore this vision of the future, which is opposed to false hopes in a return of full employment, must not lead either to a new class division between paid workers and civil workers or to the eviction of women from paid labour or the worsening of their dual burden of paid work and domestic labour. The animation of local democracy is thus bound up with the following assumptions about the division of labour in 'multi-active' society.

1 Working hours should be reduced for everyone in full-time work.
2 Every woman and every man should have one foot in paid employment if they so wish.
3 Parental labour and work with children should have the same social recognition as *civil labour* (a concept explained in detail in Chapters 8 and 9) in the arts, culture and politics – for example, through equality of entitlement to pensions and sickness benefits.
4 Simultaneous involvement in paid labour and civil labour presupposes a redistribution of family tasks between men and women. But it must be ensured that the prospect of choice is not once again illusory. In modern work society, the idea of taking years out and only later returning to work is fraught

6

with risks. Many women would like to take a break, but do not do so because they fear ending up in the 'part-time ghetto of the moving track' (Suzanne Franks).

Basically, this raises the question of how a postnational yet political civil society is possible in Europe. My answer is as follows. Only if the insecure new forms of paid employment are converted into a right to multiple work, a right to discontinuity, a right to choose working hours, a right to sovereignty over working time enshrined in collective-bargaining agreements – only then can new free spaces be secured in the coordination of work, life and political activity. Every person would thus be enabled to plan his or her own life over a period of one or more years, in its transitions between family, paid employment, leisure and political involvement, and to harmonize this with the claims and demands of others. Only then can the three principles of freedom, security and responsibility be adjusted and reaffirmed. To find a creative balance between paid work and 'the rest' (!) of life is already today the main cultural and political project – in the United States, in Europe, in Japan and elsewhere.

Nostalgia for the age of full employment is the last bastion that is being defended tooth and nail, in an effort to prevent the truly major issues of the second modernity from bursting into the open. How can the limits of growth be converted into tolerable forms of life and work? How are we to achieve a political Europe, with its own constitution and civil society, which makes it possible to flesh out the European idea of democracy for the global age? What answers beyond protectionism and indifference will countries find to migratory movements of the poor into the wealthier regions of the world? How will living and loving be possible after the gender revolution? What is the meaning of global justice? Or, more modestly: how will this become a vital issue of transnational political debate? These challenges appear too great, too intimidating. Yet in so far as the loss of work as the centre holding things together places society and democracy in danger, these questions may precisely come to form the new centre for a cosmopolitan society at once local and transnational.

Let us put this in a different way. The antithesis to the work society is not free time or a leisure society, which remain negatively imprisoned in the value imperialism of work. It is the new self-active, self-aware, political civil society – the 'do it yourself culture' – which is developing, testing and implementing a dense new concept of the political.

A method with risks

Marcel Proust was right: the true voyage of discovery is not to visit new countries but to see reality with new eyes. For social scientists, of course, there is the methodological problem of which data and arguments could ever inform a future-oriented study that breaks with the basic assumptions of the work society. This question may be answered with another. How can the present state of the fragmented and globalized work societies be properly analysed and understood *without* scenarios of possible futures?

Conventional analyses of the work society, which never raise the question of alternative futures, nevertheless imply that the biographical, social and political norms of the work society will continue indefinitely into the future. In general, there is a tacit assumption that the past and present model will also be the future model – namely, the full-employment society, with its guiding ideas, institutions, economic and political organizations, and cultural identities. When it comes to specifics, then, investigations of late work societies here rest, strictly speaking, upon an unexpressed More-of-the-Same dogma that fails to confront alternative scenarios either empirically, theoretically or politically.

This approach has long ceased to correspond to the fact that all the social sciences, including economics, are faced with the same questions and difficulties. For it is as problematic to infer the future from current trends and data as it is to read it from the tea leaves. One special source of difficulties is the fact that, given the fundamental changes in the work society, we need conceptual frameworks to identify new realities in their specificity, rather than as anomalies to be swept under the carpet of normality. This book represents one attempt to do this – which is why it belongs to the category of 'visionary non-fiction'.[5] The argument is *non-fiction* because, in describing both the present and the future state of things, it has recourse to all imaginable and available arguments, data, concepts and models. It is *visionary* because,

8

in opposition to the unexpressed self-perpetuation of the work society, it presents the embryonic vision of a post-work society whose basic features and traces can already be glimpsed today, in a new translocal and transnational sense of political civil society. The reader will be able to decide at the end whether this vision is plausible, eccentric, fantastic or realistic – or perhaps even all together.[6]

2

The Antithesis to the Work Society

Every question concerning the shape of the future must be taken to extremes – not for the sake of being radical, but in order to break down the appearance of natural and eternal self-evidence with which What-Exists armours itself against any challenge. The present needs an antithesis to clarify the reach of its dominion and the point at which something different begins. But what is the antithetical concept to the work society?

Paid work is said to be disappearing, but many think that in its place are appearing family work, parental work, ecologically purified work for the common good, or work that people really want to do. The extent to which work is part of the modern European's moral being and self-image is evident from the fact that, in Western culture, it has long been the only relevant source and the only valid measure for the evaluation of human beings and their activities. Only those things which are proven and recognized to be work count as valuable; the antithesis to the work society would appear to involve no more than an act of desertion.

Work has become so omnipotent that there is really no other concept opposed to it. Hence, any attempt to break out of this totalitarian value-circle of work lays itself open to the accusation of cynicism. For a society without work, so it seems, is a society without a centre, a society lacking basic coordinates in matters both large and small, in everyday life as in politics, economics, the law, and so on. Any vision worthy of the name must therefore cast off this spell of work, and begin by breaking the taboo on any antithesis to the work society.

The task, then, is to widen and sharpen our vista of the future beyond the work society. Only then can a systematic answer be given to the question of how far we do or do not still live in a normal work society.

Historically, we may distinguish three epochs (or better, three models) in the relationship between work and freedom, work and political action. These are (1) the Greek polis; (2) the work-democracy of the first modernity, whose ideas go back a long way but which finally became a reality only after the Second World War in Europe; and (3) the possibility of freedom and politics beyond the work society. The following sketch, highly schematic and almost irresponsibly brief, will try to do no more than clarify the radical shift in the valuation of work in the transition from Antiquity to modern times.

The Greek polis, or unfreedom through work

In ancient Greece and Rome, freedom was defined not least – in fact, primarily – as freedom from work. Anyone who had to work was not only unfree; he did not count as a member of society. For its part, society arose and consisted in public political activity. It was beyond work that the 'realm of freedom' commenced. Society was even defined as an opposite world to the world of work, filled by the art of public exchange, leisure and politics. Of course, the polis presupposed an uncomplaining realm of necessity in the shape of extra-human slave society and the repression of women. Here freedom for the few was built upon the unfreedom of the many, indeed their exclusion from society.

Modern work-democracy, or freedom through work

If work once excluded people from society, it has today become the core value and mode of integration in modern societies, to such an extent that almost no alternative remains.[7]

11

The old hierarchy of 'lower' and 'higher', of useful or necessary chores and free, meaningful, active individuality – a hierarchy expressed in many European languages in such couplets as *ponos/ergon, labor/opus* or *Mühe/Werk* – was turned around with the onset of modernity. (Or one might say, according to one's point of view, that it was turned on its head or right side up.) In this sense modernity represented a veritable revolution. People now defined themselves through the very thing that in Antiquity had meant exclusion from society: paid labour. This radical revaluation worked itself out under the aegis of the Reformation, the bourgeois revolution and political economy. The word 'industry', which gave the epoch its name in the concept of 'industrial society' coined by Saint-Simon, itself derives from the Latin *industria*, with its primary sense of industriousness. The term for the epoch was thus also combatively directed against the rule of the unproductive nobility. Labouring men began to demonize men of leisure and to subscribe to the ideology of growth. This led in turn straight into the conceptual cage of 'the realm of necessity'.

'Do some work, so that the devil always finds you occupied', one already reads in the preaching of St Jerome. This mistrust of idleness grew by leaps and bounds with the victory of the bourgeois work society. But this should not be confused with the coming of full employment. 'Historically speaking, high unemployment or underemployment was the normal case.'[8] Around 1800 roughly two-thirds of the working population, the so-called lower classes, had no regular or secure source of income. Day-labourers were probably without an income for a half or so of their working life, and up to a fifth of the able-bodied population roamed the land as beggars and vagabonds, if not as thieves and robbers.

Ivan Illich has shown in his historical studies that the revaluation of work by the bourgeoisie corresponded to a twofold innovation. The availability of paid work was supposed to be the key instrument both for the struggle against poverty and for the integration of people into the social order. Work society thus meant orderly society. And even today, those who get work also overcome poverty, drug addiction, criminality, and so on. The daily rhythm of work, with its discipline, its values and its conception

12

of personal responsibility and cooperation, corresponds to the demands made by the rulers of the work society upon their workers and employees. This demand for order within the work society is still with us today – indeed, it has become part of the self-understanding of people who form, revalue and naturalize their own identity and personality only in and through work. The biblical curse – that only they who work shall eat – has become the work morality grounding human existence; only those who work are truly human.

Thus unemployment and underemployment – or, to use the nicer-sounding modern terms, varied, fuzzy, precarious forms of work and income – were historically the rule. Moreover, there was no unemployment, because there was no norm of work. A minority had a fixed and secure place in society from which it was unusual to rise or fall. Poverty and hopelessness were the 'God-given destiny' of large numbers of people. Day-labourers, beggars and criminals constituted forms of existence often hard to distinguish from one another, which were the only means of livelihood for a sizeable part of the population.

In modern times, the idea of democracy came into the world in Europe and America as a work-democracy, in the sense that living democracy presupposed living involvement in paid labour. The citizen was conceived as a working citizen. That anyway was the political project after the Second World War, reflecting the catastrophic experience of fascism and the opposing image of Communism. Working citizens had to earn their living somehow or other, in order to give life to the political rights and freedoms. Paid labour has been the constant ground of both private and public existence. So the issue now is not 'only' the millions without work, nor 'only' the fate of the welfare state and the prevention of poverty and exclusion, but also the future of political freedom and democracy in Europe.

The Western association of capitalism with basic political, social and economic rights is by no means an 'act of philanthropy' that can be dispensed with in hard times. Rather, socially buffered capitalism is a practical application of enlightened thinking. It rests upon the insight that only people with a home and a secure job, and thus a material stake in the future, are or will become citizens who make democracy their own and breathe real life into it. The simple truth is that without material security there can be no political freedom – hence no democracy, but rather a threat to everyone from new and old totalitarian regimes and ideologies.

The future of work and political action

Quite clearly the work society is reaching its technological and ecological limits. This reintroduces a paradox that was once decisive for the development of the work society: on the one hand, work is the centre of society around which everything and everyone revolve and take their bearings; on the other hand, everything is done to eliminate as much work as possible. Productivity, to be worthy of the name, means the removal of more and more human labour, yet this sets off and establishes a dynamic in which the *vita activa*, if not yet superfluous, loses its central meaning. Such are the paradoxes of the work-centred society.

'Is your company planning to expand with the help of new products?' Hoechst chairman Jürgen Dormann is asked. 'Will that also mean new jobs?' – 'No,' he answers. – 'So where are the new jobs being created, if it is not in high-tech pharmaceuticals?' – 'That's a good question.' And Dormann adds: 'I don't go along any more with all these hypocritical flourishes. Our aim is to keep employment at today's levels. To do even that we'll have to be extremely successful.'

New discoveries, new or at least restructured knowledge, are being deployed on a scale and at a speed that would be appropriate to a new natural resource.

Just as, in the transition from hunter-gatherer to agrarian society, people began to think of the earth they had wandered since time immemorial as a natural resource, or just as, in the transition from agrarian to industrial society, fossil energy sources going back millions of years began to play a completely new role, so is man's knowledge acquiring a new quality from the changed premises of his formation, networking and reconversion. Man, of course, has always used knowledge to make his work easier, but in the past it was only as an aid. Now knowledge is taking the place of working people, and people are enlisted in the service of knowledge. The relationship has been reversed between fluid labour in the shape of human beings and labour that has flowed away in the shape of knowledge. Both inside and outside the human brain, knowledge accounts for a fast-growing proportion of value creation.[9]

There is a sneaking concern, however, that the work ethos which helped capitalism to victory is based upon an inadequate view of automation; or, worse still, that a fear of freedom is expressed in the attempts of late work society to regain the lost paradise of full employment. This can be seen in matters both large and small. Everywhere the quest is now on for labour-intensive forms of production and services. What most catches the eye is the low productivity of certain branches of production, and the so-called 'simple' services such as cleaning, looking after dogs and children and taking them for a walk, shopping and other activities which, in Europe at least, have long been performed by various members of the family. The fear of freedom, or so it would seem, is thus resorting to a protectionist policy of holding down productivity. It is the language used in calls for 'simple services', marked by low productivity and low wages, although a role is also certainly played by the suspicion of late work society that its model of order and its morality of rule are as antiquated as those of knights in shining armour or medieval guilds.

At the same time, a new model is taking shape in Germany in which the struggle against unemployment draws upon various liberal, Green and communitarian sources. The basic idea behind this project is a dual-activity (or multi-activity) society. The aim is no longer to regain full employment in the classical sense, in which freedom, political action and democracy were at once facilitated, dominated and circumscribed by paid labour. Rather, it is – as André Gorz puts it – 'to capture, alongside and beyond the apparatus logic, greater spaces of autonomy . . . that permit a fairly unrestricted blossoming of individual existence'.[10] Here the political goal will be defined as something that is (also) possible: namely, to open up and secure new spaces in which a variety of activities – family work and public-civil labour – are able to develop.

So long as this does not mean a mere redistribution of scarcity – 'Men forward to the stove!' or some such motto – we can see here the makings of a real vision. With the end of the work society, the mood of doom and gloom resulting from technological advances

15

in labour productivity and from the awareness of ecological destruction can be turned around into the beginnings of a self-active political society.

Before we again take up the question of the future scenarios of work, we should clarify the framework and points of reference for the existing debate.

3

The Transition from the First to the Second Modernity

Five Challenges

'Second modernity' is a magical password that is meant to open the door to new conceptual landscapes. On all sides, the great volcanic questions continue to bubble beneath the surface. If the full employment society has come to an end, then we must eventually face up to the collapse of pensions due to the imbalance between a shrinking labour force and the ever larger and older numbers of the elderly. At the same time, the whole conceptual world of national sovereignty is fading away – a world that includes the taming of capitalism in Europe by the postwar welfare state. That densely knit institutional structure may be retrospectively termed the 'first modernity' – as opposed to a 'second modernity' whose contours are still unclear. This distinction will help us avoid the 'protectionist reflex' that has had such a numbing effect in Europe, both intellectually and politically, since the collapse of the bipolar world order. For the economic prosperity of a more or less stable social order lasted for just a tiny speck of eternity, and there is no reason at all to think that after it social change and social history have come to a complete stop. Today, in the wake of 'reflexive modernization', change is affecting a whole range of aspects that used to function alongside one another: the neocorporatist bargaining systems, the company forms of work and production, the mass parties deeply rooted in the social structure, the fallback systems of social security,

17

the small families with a traditional division of labour between men and women, the standardized working conditions and career trajectories. All these are being challenged in what Habermas calls the new 'postnational constellation'.

What I have called the 'first modernity', then, was characterized by collective lifestyles, full employment, the national state and the welfare state, and an attitude of heedless exploitation of nature. The second modernity, on the other hand, is characterized by ecological crises, the decline of paid employment, individualization, globalization and gender revolution. The relationship between the first and the second modernity presents two problems, however. The first problem is that although the guiding ideas or coordinates of change seem ultra-stable, they are in fact themselves undergoing change. But the central scientific and political problem of the second modernity is that societies must respond to such changes at all levels at once. In the end, therefore, it is illusory to debate the future of work without also discussing the future of the nation-state, the welfare state, and so on. Yet this is also an age in which postmodernism and systems theory have announced the end of politics, when what I have called 'freedom's children' seem to be giving up any kind of politics or protest action, adrift from any tradition or perspectives for the future.

Against such intellectual retreat, those who base their theories on the concept of a second modernity argue instead for the realism of a pessimistic optimism. For anyone today who diagnoses collapse without new openings is blind. And anyone who speaks of new openings without recognizing the collapse is naive.

What is meant by 'reflexive modernization'?

'Modernization' is a magical word, one which for many people conveys the idea of Americanization, Europeanization, Westernization – in short, imperialism. The little word 'reflexive' does not seem to help much in this respect. Indeed, to initiates, the phrase 'reflexive modernization' sounds almost tautological. For does not modernization always involve reflection about modernization?

From the First to the Second Modernity

Nevertheless, both these responses are based on a major misconception. 'Reflexive modernization' does not mean reflection about the consequences of modernization; nor does it mean the Eurocentrism of the old politics of modernization. The term 'reflexive modernization' puts the central focus on the self-transformation and opening up of the first, national modernity – processes which have, for the most part, been unintended and unforeseen. What it signals is no longer change *in* society, but change *of* society, of the whole of society – or, to be more precise, change affecting the foundations of whole modern societies.

In the past, a change of society was associated with revolutions. This meant a number of things. First, new elites were ready to impose themselves. Second, new social doctrines or political utopias clashed with theories and actors who defended the old system of domination. Third, political alternatives took shape under pressure from below; whether from the liberal bourgeoisie at the time of the Enlightenment, John Locke and Adam Smith; or from the proletariat in the movement associated with Marx, Engels and Lenin. Fourth, clear lines of conflict emerged, which then took an acute political form.

None of these features applies to the concept of 'reflexive modernization', which points instead to change on the basis of radical, accelerated modernization. There are no new elites coming up from below, nor new social utopias or clear lines of conflict. On the contrary, the changes in question take place *despite* the fact that they are to the disadvantage of large majorities and to the advantage only of elite minorities (the 'global players', for example). But they are certainly powerful changes, even though no one set them as a political goal, and even though they have not been the object of adequate public debate or political decision. How has this come about? The key factor has been the dynamic power of technological and economic innovation within the framework of global capitalism. This dynamism, championed and released by the movement we know as neoliberalism, has been revolutionizing the very foundations of society. The term 'reflexive modernization', then, refers to the transition away from a first modernity locked within the national state, and towards a second, open, risk-filled modernity characterized by general insecurity. This transition takes place, as it were, within a continuity of 'capitalist modernization', which is now in the process of removing the fetters of the national and the welfare state.

From the First to the Second Modernity

Although the concept of a first modernity goes back a long way, its densely knit institutional structure only took shape in the great transformation of postwar Europe. Besides, the first modernity should be understood as a characteristically 'halfway modernity'. In its model of industrial society, basic principles of modernity are unthinkingly assumed as, so to speak, 'corporatist' premises. We might list seven such premises:

1 each country's organization of its own 'national' economy;
2 widespread exclusion of women from the labour market;
3 the withholding of certain basic rights from women and children;
4 the existence of intact small families as the basis for the reproduction of labour-power as a chiefly male commodity;
5 relatively closed proletarian and bourgeois lifeworlds as the social or 'status' precondition of class formation;
6 a hierarchy of experts and laymen based upon professionally generated and supervised monopolies of knowledge; and
7 geographically fixed production, cooperation and company activity – as the supposedly 'natural' arena in which the contradictions of labour and capital both appear and become susceptible to organization and pacification.

These are 'basic premises' in another sense, too. For they are seen throughout society as institutionally and individually self-evident – as a kind of 'second nature'. Thus, in the model of the first modernity, any claim to universality is restricted by axioms of social difference and fencing. These axioms are, in essence, based upon supposedly 'natural' categories – for example, on the distinction between men and women or children and adults, or on a national organization of the economy, or on the availability of nature itself as an exploitable 'resource'. Things change, however, with the triumph of universalism in economics as well as in law and society – which is to say, in people's attitudes and in the life-plans they consider normal. Now the infinite space of the first modernity is breaking up. The individualization process, for example, condenses expectations of a 'life of one's own' – expectations generated and internalized through the successive incorporation of the whole population into the educational system and the labour market. This gives rise to what Habermas calls a 'new obscurity' in the cultural foundations of society (right down to the ways in which we think of love and intimacy). The organizers and (sociological) interpreters of the society of individuals are thus confronted with more and more new puzzles.

In the second modernity, the process of modernization is reflexive in the sense that it has increasingly to face unintended and unwanted consequences of its own success. This means that boundaries tend to break down, as social conditions which 'spontaneously' framed the first modernity disappear in the wake of further modernization. Here are a few examples of what I have in mind.

1 The corporatist internal structure of classes, and therefore of class society as a whole, tends to fade as social inequalities increase.
2 Openly debated ecological crises make the public more alive to the cultural perception and evaluation of 'nature'.
3 Sexual and inter-generational relations between men and women, adults and children are stripped of their basic pseudo-natural premise, so that a gradual revolution affects the whole world of the small family, with its conceptions of the division of labour, love and home life.
4 The society of formal work and full employment, as well as the welfare-state nexus associated with it, enter into crisis as production and cooperation lose their clearly defined local ties.
5 The imaginative world of a private sphere, in the sense of 'normal biographies' exclusively geared to market opportunities, becomes political again.
6 The experience of global risks to civilization calls into question the traditional rule by experts in economics, politics and science. Basic democratic movements, with their claims to technocratic citizenship, are thus released into the public debate of experts and counter-experts.

To express this in a metaphor, we are dealing here with a 'revolution of side-effects'.[11] Concepts such as 'ambivalence', 'unclarity' or 'contradictoriness', but also others such as 'disorientation', seem to become more not less significant as the changes take effect. Who should be asked for what? How is the new situation to be defined? Who might be the 'subject' of badly needed reforms? The questions have come to appear stronger than any answers.

Perhaps this is actually the key point. The first modernity gave a series of institutionalized answers to the problems facing society: more and better technology, more and better scientific research, more and better functional differentiation. But these answers no longer convince us; they no longer engage with the situation. For contemporary societies are going through a fundamental transformation which radically challenges the understanding of modernity rooted in the European Enlightenment. The field of reference is now made up of many different options, and new, unexpected forms of the social and the political are emerging within this field.

In the 1990s, debates in social science began to get to grips with this emergence of new forms, and with the sweeping away of old forms of the social and the political. Some used the concept of 'postmodernity' to denote a moral-political, late-feminist turn (Lyotard, Harvey, Haraway, Bauman, Sennett). Others speak of 'reflexive modernization' (Beck, Giddens and Lash) or of a 'third way' (Giddens and others). A large circle has formed around the concepts of 'cultural globalization' and 'glocalization' (Robertson, Featherstone, Lash, Urry, and others). A further key author is Arjun Appadurai, with his concepts of 'ethnoscape' and 'global flows'. Martin Albrow's 'global age' belongs here, as do the concepts of a 'knowledge and information society' (Drucker, Castells, Latour, Knorr-Cetina) and of a 'postnational constellation' (Habermas). All these positions have three things in common.

First, they share a theoretical and political 'anti-Thatcherism'. For it was Margaret Thatcher who declared that only the state, the market and the family really existed; that there was no such thing as society. And she lost no time in trying to make this come true politically. We may say that the devastating consequences of that political programme paved the way for Tony Blair's rapid ascent. And the avant-garde social science of the 1990s also took up arms against that structural (not necessarily intended) nexus of postmodernism, Thatcherism and neoliberalism, which involved the denial or abolition of society and politics.

Second, all the sociological currents in question agree that the future is becoming more open. However different their ideas in other respects, they all argue that the human condition at the end of the twentieth century holds out fundamentally ambivalent prospects – prospects marked by uncertainty, paradox and risk.

Third, all these authors consider that hope and despair are two sides of the same phenomenon. Alongside and against the rhetoric of collapse and crisis, they all allow space in their theory for new beginnings and a process of restructuring. They thus try to develop new categories, new coordinates, new spatial and temporal determinations of the social and the political. One central question binds them together. What begins to happen when the contours, foundations and lines of conflict of the first modernity grow blurred and disappear? I have developed in a number of places my own answer to this question of what begins to happen. It is that modernity becomes differentiated between a first modernity based on the national state, and a second modernity in which boundaries tend to vanish.

Such a distinction requires two further questions to be answered. What is the basis of the continuity between the first and the second modernity? And what is the basis of their discontinuity? The distinction is not that the second modernity knows ruptures, collapses and crises, whereas the first modernity does not know them. Indeed, it is a basic feature of modernity as such that antinomies and conflicts are built into the political order of societies. For there is no pre-established harmony between the various elements of modern society: between the values that legitimate a social and political order, the institutionalized form of rule, the different sub-systems and socio-economic interests, the winners and losers from innovation and change, and the claims of individuals to a life of their own. There is always something provisional about modern society: it is always imperfect and conflictual, always shot through with contingency and complexity. And it is our understanding of this which is made more open and sharply focused by the rational tools of social science.

The distinction between a first and a second modernity should not be misunderstood in another way either. It does not mean that the questions of globalization, individualization, gender revolution, job insecurity and ecological crisis are addressed in the second modernity but not in the first modernity. The key point is rather *how* these questions are perceived and tackled.

The epochal change is based on the fact that the guiding ideas and core institutional responses of the first modernity no longer appear self-evident or even convincing. This is true of the idea of territoriality in relation to globalization; it is true of full employment in relation to the work society; it is true of fixed ideas of community and hierarchy in relation to individualization; it is true of a 'natural' division of labour between men and women in relations between the sexes; and it is true of limitless growth through the exploitation of nature, in relation to the ecological crisis. A crucial result follows from this. The West's guiding ideas about modernity, and its claims even to have a monopoly on modernity, are in the process of falling apart.

In the model of the first modernity, everything is constantly changing – but not the basic categories and concepts of social change itself. In the second modernity, however, these categories and concepts are openly challenged – above all, the conviction that there is ultimately a rational solution for every problem that modernization itself produces. This challenge takes place both at the level of institutions and at the level of discourse. For the paradigm shift from the first to the second modernity also polarizes and politicizes groups within society, and it does so in the shape of a conflict between the two modernities. At the same time, however, social science is faced with a challenge to revise its own theories. As Max Weber already saw, when the light of the great value issues and world problems moves on, social scientists too must review and restock their apparatus of concepts.

This theory-guided change in perspective between the first and the second modernity must now be briefly illustrated with regard to globalization.

Globalization, or the 'despatialization of the social'

In the paradigm of the first modernity, 'simple' globalization is interpreted within the territorial compass of state and politics, society and culture. This gives us a picture with the following elements.

1   There is growing external interdependence between national societies.

2   Over and above this, as it were, transnational institutions and actors are taking shape.
3   'Multicultural' identities disturb the order of state-organized national societies conceived as relatively homogeneous 'monolithic blocs'.
4   This view of globalization as an '*inter*-national', '*inter*-state' and '*inter*-societal' phenomenon of ever greater moulding and networking does not question, but rather confirms, the distinctions between first and third world, tradition and modernity.

All these elements involve an additive, not substitutive, conception of globalization. They presuppose the territorial principle whereby spatially defined states and societies are both inwardly and outwardly quite clearly demarcated from one another.

Crucially, globalization appears in this paradigm as a process coming from without: it does admittedly undermine and perhaps wash away the political-moral-economic 'underworld' upon which modern national states support themselves, but only because the territoriality of the social and the political is not itself questioned. The result is that 'world society' is conceived as a mosaic of national societies in which the various 'stones', each relatively monolithic and integrated, constitute geopolitical spaces that 'add up' to a sum total of nations. World society is here a society of societies, which contains in itself all the national-territorial social blocs but, for that very reason, never amounts to an independent presence transcending them. This conception of globalization is 'simple' and 'linear', because it accepts largely without question the basic premise of territoriality and applies it to the very globalization which calls that basic premise into question.

Two further assumptions underlie 'simple' globalization. First, the relationship between transnational and national actors or spaces is conceived as a zero-sum game: that which is won transnationally – sovereignty, military decision-making power, democratic qualities – must be lost by the national space. It might almost be said that the transnational here appears as an enemy 'of the third kind'. Globalization threatens national sovereignty and the identity of the 'homeland', but it does so not through open rivalry, conquest or subjugation but by 'subversively' intensifying economic dependence, transnational decision-making powers and multicultural influences.

Second, this territorial conception of globalization goes together with a substantialist-essentialist misunderstanding of society, culture, nation and identity. In this sense, the greatest difference between the New World and the Old World is that, in most of the lands of Europe, people think they have always been there. Myths of national origin are quite recent, however, mostly 'invented' (in the true sense of the word) in the eighteenth and nineteenth centuries. Even the national symbol of Scotland, the kilt, originated from an English producer of fabrics and clothing.

In the paradigm of the second, reflexive modernity, globalization changes not only the relations between and beyond national states and social blocs, but also the inner quality of the social itself. What goes to make up 'society' or 'politics' becomes intrinsically questionable, because the principle of territoriality becomes questionable. To be more precise, the posited overlap of state and society is cancelled and transcended, as ever more forms of economic and social action, work and life cease to be acted out within the containing framework of the state.

The core of globalization is here seen as deterritorialization of the social. Economics, politics and lifestyles do not only push their way across the old national frontiers; they change their position within them too. More and more things happen not just simultaneously but in the same place, without any preparation in our thinking and action for the collapse of distance. Suddenly the world is getting cramped – not because of population growth, but because of the cultural effect that seems to be inexorably drawing the remote and alien closer together. The Indian-American anthropologist Arjun Appadurai has also noted the reverse phenomenon: namely, the continued cultural distance and foreignness of fellow-citizens and neighbours who, having come as immigrants to the West, do not abandon the media-supported 'ethnic space' that allows them still to live in their virtual homeland.

In the paradigm of the second modernity, then, a question mark is placed over the inner consistency of a social construction made up of anthropological constants and functional imperatives of the first modernity. A territorially fixed image of the social, which for two centuries has captivated and inspired the political, cultural

26

and scientific imagination, is in the course of breaking up. Corresponding to global capitalism is a process of cultural and political globalization which transcends territoriality as the ordering principle of society (and as the ordering principle of cultural knowledge upon which familiar images of the self and the world are based).

Capital is global, work is local

The meaning of this deterritorialization or despatialization of the social and the political can best be illustrated by the example of economic activity and the associated future of work. The global economy rests upon the capacity to eat up distance and to organize in real time a fragmented labour process into a planetary whole. The result is a change in the inner structure of society, in its categorial architecture. In nation-based continental Europe, labour, capital and state worked with and against one another as collective actors, in accordance with the corporatist model of 'organizational power'; each followed the rules in negotiating its share of the 'economic cake' of gross domestic product. But in the transnational power game, this territorially based power of organizations is circumvented and replaced by something like a transnational power of withdrawal.[12] This is superior to organizational power, because it operates not just 'in area' but in the wider 'space' of transnational power. It therefore applies even where globalization has not yet become 'actual' (for example, through foreign investment or transnational trade relations), but is already seen as a possibility dictating what appears on the pages of newspapers and in people's heads. In this way, the publicly staged rhetoric of globalization is also a discursive strategy that can display the power of a self-fulfilling prophecy.

Economic processes lose their fixed spatial attachment, which once seemed an inescapable condition of work in industrial society. Geographical distance thus loses much of its significance as a 'natural' limit to competition between different production sites. In the 'distanceless' space of computer technology, every location in the world now potentially competes with all others for scarce capital investment and cheap supplies of labour.

The power relations between labour and capital become sharper as they are thus relocated within the structure of space and time.

27

This may be expressed in a single formula: labour is local, capital is global. It is a social-spatial power difference which corresponds to an epochal gap in organizational qualities: capital is globally coordinated, labour is individualized. Conflicts between diversified interests of capital and virtual working classes remain bound up with the opposition between the logic of unbounded capital flows and the fragmented horizons of experience.

The internationalization of production thus offers companies at least two strategic advantages: global competition breaks out between high-priced and low-priced labour; and the fiscal conditions and controls of individual states can be played off against one another and undermined. One may see in this new power of transnational corporations a successful transfer of market laws to the sphere of politics. But the reality is much more pungent than that. Since claims on numerous public services (universities, hospitals, transport, courts, research funds) are not tied to the place where taxes are raised, many companies are in a position to minimize their fiscal burden, while at the same time setting up shop in countries that offer the best infrastructure.

A decision may indeed be taken for the locations of investment, production, tax-payment and corporate headquarters to be in four different countries. Many companies use the lower taxation of poor states and take advantage of the higher living standards of rich states. They pay taxes where they are lowest, and live where it is nicest. They become free riders profiting from expensive infrastructural development.

The resulting state of the world may perhaps be ironically expressed in the following image. In the time of the first modernity, capital, labour and state played at baking cakes in nationally defined and organized sand-pits, and they did indeed succeed in baking them according to all the rules of 'institutionalized conflict'. But now, suddenly, the economy has been given an excavator and is clearing the whole sand-pit away. Trade union leaders and politicians sit there in a huff and cry out for help.

Localization of globalization

In the paradigm of the second modernity, then, globalization is no longer understood as external and additive, but replaces the 'container image' of society and the state. It designates a transnational, despatialized power game, whose rules and boundaries, paradoxes and dilemmas, first have to be deciphered. Already we can see the outlines of the paradox of social closeness and geographical distance: that is, geographically remote differences and oppositions are lived and experienced as socially proximate, whereas geographical proximity leaves untouched the differentness of social worlds. People can exist in one and the same place as if they were on different planets, while continents merge into a single social space in which people may live together across vast distances.

This can be seen most clearly in the metropolises of the world market – London, New York, Tokyo, Hong Kong, São Paulo, Paris, Frankfurt, and so on – which, as Saskia Sassen suspects, show us the future of the city.[13] Here the assembled world problems take people's breath away, not only literally. For the real novelty is that urban districts, firms, occupational groups, and thus millions of individuals of every skin colour and religion, live and work in both local isolation and global association with one another. The paradox of social proximity and geographical distance thus takes shape in a social-spatial figure: local disintegration amid global integration.

As studies of the success of Silicon Valley in the 1990s have shown, extra-regional and trans-regional relations play a key role for technological-economic 'cultures of innovation'. In this sense, argues Richard Gordon, localized arrangements must enable regional corporations and economic actors to participate in the global network of regional economic spaces.[14]

Large and small firms, one-person businesses and world corporations, if they want to operate globally, must therefore first do the same thing: develop a localization strategy. In other words, globalization presupposes localization – though in a different kind of social-spatial calculus, because that which used to be tied together in a single place can now stretch across the globe and yet still work as one cooperative unit. Accordingly there are globalized 'patterns of localization' – most clearly in the case of American corporate cultures.

1 Research and innovation take place in industrial centres with a high quality of life.
2 Skilled production is established in the 'home' country –

29

which, in the case of the United States, means in medium-sized cities in the western states.

3   Production sites that require medium skill levels are largely transferred overseas – for example, to South-East Asia, including Singapore and Malaysia.

4   Sales, marketing and administration are sited in regional centres around the world, mostly within large electronic industrial estates.

Mobility or migration

The change in perspective between the first and the second modernity, between national and postnational modernity, may also be illustrated by the (ambiguous) understanding of 'migration' and 'mobility' between and within individual countries. In the nation-state paradigm of the first modernity, there was a razor-sharp distinction between 'migration' and 'mobility' – indeed, opposite values were typically assigned to the two. Population shifts within a national state meant mobility and were highly desired, especially in view of regional imbalances in the labour market. Part of the ideal of the 'flexible worker' is that he or she should go where the jobs are. The fact that this breaks up families, because wives and mothers are also economically active and must display 'flexibility', is studiously avoided by those who are apologists for both market and family.

Mobility between national states, on the other hand, is regarded as 'migration' and subjected to major restrictions. At the border posts, 'desirable flexibility' thus turns into 'undesirable migration', and people who do what is so much demanded within individual countries find themselves being criminalized. They are 'economic refugees', 'asylum-seekers' or 'illegal immigrants', who put themselves in the hands of 'human traffickers' – a task discharged within each country by the official employment exchange. How can citizens who believe in universalist values and rights become, within a transnational dimension, enemies of the very mobility for which they insistently call inside their own country?

Globalization, understood as despatialization of the social, opens up a new analytical framework and new strategic options. If one removes, at least hypothetically, the restrictions of the national state, three scenarios emerge for the post-national distribution of work and wealth.

1 *Global population shifts.* It is thought by many that growing worldwide inequalities, as well as differences between the less highly populated rich countries of the North and the more highly populated poor countries of the South, will trigger new population shifts towards parts of the world with an attractive standard of living.
2 *Migration of labour.* Others argue that it is not people but jobs (and suitable training opportunities) which will migrate – to overpopulated regions where the poor and unemployed live.
3 *Transnational job-sharing between poor and rich countries.* In this scenario, new ways of sharing work and riches across frontiers and continents will emerge without migration. Through the abolition of distance made possible by production based on information technology, a post-national distribution of work and riches might be achieved in the long term, in which less-skilled jobs will be exported from the rich to the poor countries. At the same time, jobs requiring more skills will be established in countries with a relatively low population density but a high average level of skills.

In the first of these scenarios, seen in the West as the nightmare scenario, the metaphor of a supposedly full boat stirs up fear and hatred of foreigners. The second has already been happening for a long time – some twenty years or so – but it encounters strong resistance on the part of governments and trade unions in the 'job-exporting' countries.

The third scenario, international job-sharing, deserves very serious public discussion as an alternative to mass emigration or Western protectionism. As David Elkins argues, the despatialization of the social raises two opposing questions. If it is true that transnational societies and a corresponding division of labour are taking shape, and that this includes a redistribution of life chances, will the pressure to emigrate therefore lessen? And if – to follow this idea through – corporations recruit their employees from everywhere, will this not do away with the need to seek one's happiness on other continents? In other words, if territoriality no longer defines a person's identity and life chances, why should he or she decide to emigrate?[15]

Exactly the opposite question can also be asked, however. If territoriality is less and less important for social relations and social proximity, why should émigrés continue to be regarded as émigrés and not welcomed as mobile workers? If a pattern of social relations develops in which transnational, 'despatialized' social networks and 'sociospheres' (Martin Albrow) are the dominant feature, and people live their lives across frontiers in communities of their own choosing, why should they be prevented from emigrating to wherever they wish to live?

The key question, then, is the extent to which post-national forms of the division of labour and wealth will be developed in the transnational constellation. In so far as this occurs, the protectionist double morality that distinguishes between desirable mobility and undesirable migration will lose its meaning. The idea of (both spatial and cultural) mobility – which was originally associated with modernity – is now triggered by the pressures of geographical labour mobility and transfers of wealth. Its distinctive cultural meaning may thus be elucidated and verified anew, and in the process it may be possible to scale down spatial mobility and the resulting transport chaos.[16]

Two things become clear from this example. First, we can see how important it is in the paradigm of the second modernity to raise the question of the future of work at once transnationally and post-nationally. Just to continue thinking within the old schema of work specialization, and to ask how the 'cancer of unemployment' can be finally overcome, is to remain trapped within the major misconceptions of the national paradigm of the first modernity.

Second, it becomes apparent that a new division of labour between economics and politics is establishing itself in the second modernity. Willy-nilly the economy is becoming the locus and arm of transnational politics. Corporations shape the living conditions and situation of people in world society – mostly unobserved, with many prejudices and so far exclusively in their own economic interests. Much in the future will depend on whether, under public regulation, they are responsible and politically controllable in their increased capacity to mould transnational space. What is the basis of this transnational corporate 'politics'? Part of the answer is that corporate policies help to create the foundations for equality, justice, freedom and democracy on a world scale, because their investment decisions are central to the distribution of work and income. The premises of a transnational democracy can be established only if there is cooperation between transnationally enlarged, state-organized politics and a responsible economics conscious of its political action within world society.

When the frontiers blur: beyond war and peace?

The territoriality principle should not, however, be confused with the territorial or national state, nor with the social state built upon the same foundations. But in so far as the overcoming of the territoriality principle, through a kind of domino effect, abolishes the basic premises of this state formation, a number of further points need to be made by way of clarification.

Territorial states originate in exclusive powers over geographical space. This is the basis for their monopoly of violence, their legislative autonomy, cultural identity and moral autonomy; the basis too for civil rights, and for decisions about who may be included in or excluded from them. The following phenomena and basic questions will show that this multifunctionality of the principle of territorial organization for politics and society has developed and split in the transition to the second modernity.

1 *Loss of sovereignty and renationalization.* After the collapse of the bipolar East-West conflict, nationalist movements and sentiments burst forth on all sides – not only in Europe, but in the Arab states, Africa, and so on. But this nationalist upsurge should be clearly distinguished from the institutional sovereignty of national states in the formation of political blocs within the world system. Here a paradoxical connection may be observed between the weakening of national power and sovereignty and the sharpening of nationalist orientations and currents. It is also worth noting that the one becomes the 'cause' of the other.

2 *Subnational and transnational nations.* Many countries of Africa or other regions of the so-called third world may be under-

stood as 'quasi-states', in the sense that they combine external sovereignty with failing internal control. The result is a politically and socially precarious structure of partial societies and identities, in terms of both inward and outward reference. The political vitality of what might be called 'subnational and transnational nations', such as the Palestinians, Kurds, Catalans, Scots or Quebecois, should be warning enough that 'national states' belonging to the United Nations are being effectively challenged by 'would-be nations' struggling for territory and international recognition.

3 *Intervention in the 'internal affairs' of other states*. Denationalization is also visible in a growing preparedness for outside intervention in the 'internal affairs' of states – on the part of both the subject and the object of intervention. The most obvious example of this are the conditions imposed by the World Bank (for countries in Africa, Asia and South America, but also for Russia). But the same trend can be seen in disputes over whether developed countries have a moral and political duty to write off the debts of developing countries – or whether, on the contrary, this would be economic lunacy. 'Foreign intervention' has also become an accepted notion in debates about the prevention of humanitarian and ecological catastrophes. The same is true of the activities of Amnesty International, Greenpeace, the PEN Club and many other non-governmental, transnational actors and organizations – to say nothing of drug cartels, terrorists and fundamentalist religious movements.

4 *War and peace*. The national state linked the exercise of force to the distinction between within and without. Internally it established a violence-free space as the precondition for democratic equality among competing ethnic, religious and economic classes and interest groups. Against perceived external dangers, however, there was a readiness to mobilize and employ military force. Today, with the erosion of the autonomy of the national state, and especially of its territorial control over the use of the means of violence, one architecture of the political is breaking up. The classical distinctions between 'war and peace', 'internal and external', 'public and private', 'civil society and anarchy', are in danger of falling apart.[17] But what is appearing in their place? Does it signify that the world is drifting towards a state – already glimpsed in the barbaric 'ethnic cleansing' in the former Yugoslavia – where war and civil war, anarchy and normality, are hardly distinguishable from each other? Is the world

beyond sovereign national states one in which civic life and anarchy start to become two sides of the same coin?

> Theory and politics of the second age of modernity has to anticipate powerful tensions, profound contradictions and perplexing paradoxes. It is to confront processes that mask both growth and decay. It is to look for authorities that are obscure, boundaries that are in flux, and systems of rule that are emergent. And it is to experience hope embedded in despair.[18]

4

The Future of Work and Its Scenarios

An Interim Balance-Sheet

The debate on the future of work resembles a labyrinth. Adapting an idea of Bertolt Brecht's, we might say: there are as many scenarios and questions as there are authors. So how can the future of work in the second modernity be analysed in a systematic manner?

To bring a certain clarity into this bustling international debate, it makes sense to draw a fundamental distinction between the framework of scenario-building and the challenges of the second modernity. Most of the scenarios revolve around the question of Yes or No, end or recovery of full employment, hopes and worries. And all the time, the leitmotifs of the second modernity – science-based information technology, globalization, individualization and ecological crisis – need to be analysed in their consequences for the future of work. Let us first distinguish the following scenarios within the framework of the full-employment society.

If the framework of a full-employment society is replaced with that of a multi-activity society, the collapse scenarios become the occasion for a redefinition of work and of the necessary reforms. Three more future scenarios can then be developed, as questions are raised concerning the distribution between work and activity and the provision of a secure existence. These are:

The Future of Work and its Scenarios

Table 1 Future scenarios of work

	Hope	*Collapse*
Science-based information technologies	1 From the work society to the knowledge society	2 Capitalism without work
Globalization	3 The world market – the neoliberal jobs miracle	4 The fixed location of work – a globalization risk
Ecological crises	5 Sustainable work – the ecological economic miracle	6 Global apartheid
Individualization	7 The self-employed – the freedom of insecurity	8 Individualization of work – disintegration of society

9 Farewell to the work society: instead, the multi-activity society.
10 Condemned to leisure: the free-time society.
11 Post-national and political civil society: a European social model.

The final scenario will be presented in the two concluding chapters of this book. But now the other scenarios must be successively outlined and distinguished from one another.

All models (only a few of whose basic features can be sketched here) have one thing in common: they make a case for 'reforms'. The 'reformers', for their part, base their political opposition upon conflicting accounts of the present state of the work society – for even when the adversaries belong to the same society, they live in different worlds. Here the main dividing line is between those who think that full employment will be possible in the future – provided a few levers and screws are properly adjusted – and those who rule this out.

To avoid misunderstandings, the point is not that the work society will run out of work. It is not the end of paid work but the end of full employment which is at issue. Two per cent unemployment, social security in work, normal work relations as the usual case – is all this history? So the basic dispute is over whether the full-employment society has ended for ever or will one day come back.

Scenario 1: from the work society to the knowledge society

Many authors chase away, as if it were a troublesome fly, the human concern that the revolutionary rationalization based on information technology is designed, if not to eliminate, then to thin out paid employment. Two basic elements here reinforce each other: the way in which economists think in terms of models (some would say: their model Platonism); and the historical experience of the first modernity, in which the workers' fears that they would be replaced by machines proved for long to be unfounded.

The conceptual framework of classical economics excludes in principle the notion that the work society could run out of paid jobs. In the model of *homo oeconomicus*, only certain prevailing conditions – too high a price for labour, fossilized bureaucratic structures, state intervention – can hinder the creation of new jobs. The historical variant of a capitalism without work does not even come into consideration.

It is also true that, while all previous secular leaps in development have eradicated certain types of work (in agriculture, for example), the losses have been made up through new types of work (in industry and services, for example). For the model Platonists, then, the fear that communications technology will eliminate paid employment confuses the end of old-style labour in industry and services with the end of the full-employment society as such. It is a vision which blinds people to the transformation of the national work

38

society of the first modernity into the transnational work society of the second modernity, with its new, 'delocalized' understanding of work, production and cooperation. In other words, the global information age does revolutionize the face of work – for example, by replacing unskilled work tied to a particular place with highly mobile knowledge work – but in the end a different work society will take shape in which everyone has the opportunity to find a job that gives them a living. So, it will not be less but more of a work society.

The historical period that fits best with this view was the early phase of industrial modernity in Europe. In Britain, for instance, the number of people economically active in agriculture fell dramatically between 1780 and 1988, and from 50 per cent to 2.2 per cent of all paid employment. At the same time, labour productivity soared by a factor of 68, and there was a huge accompanying consolidation of first the industrial sector and then services, which allowed a growing working-age population to be integrated into the labour market. The history of paid employment in all of the early industrialized countries looks similar right up to the 1970s. In the United States, dramatic technological change in the twentieth century led to a sweeping reduction in the numbers engaged in agriculture, but the total number of jobs in the US economy shot up from approximately 27 million in 1900 to 124.5 million in 1993.

In the last thirty years, this huge rise in the working population has been attributable not least to the 'revolutionary' increase in female employment. Between 1970 and 1990, the integration of women into the labour market climbed from 48.9 per cent to 69.1 per cent in the United States, from 55.4 per cent to 61.8 per cent in Japan, from 48.1 per cent to 61.3 per cent in Germany, from 50.8 per cent to 65.3 per cent in Great Britain, from 47.5 per cent to 59 per cent in France, from 33.5 per cent to 43.3 per cent in Italy, and from 29.2 per cent to 42.8 per cent in Spain.[19] And this surge of women into paid employment did not lead to higher male unemployment in the United States, Japan or Western Europe.

This position taken by labour-market optimists should not be confused with the views of those who, for whatever reason, hope and bet on the stability or salvation of the status quo. Indeed, it allows for the fact that whole branches of the economy are being wiped out – for example, mining, textiles and the steel industry –

and that mass redundancies will be as necessary as deep cuts in the social security system. But there is supposed to be light at the end of the tunnel of these painful frictions and encroachments. Once the necessary 'adjustments' have been made to the world market and new information technologies, the earthly paradise of the full employment society will again beckon with its inexhaustible inventiveness and its rising prosperity for all.

What is proposed by such theorists, then, is an 'evolutionary leap' that will offer protection for the future. Just as, in the transition from traditional society to the first modernity, the agricultural sector contracted and industry and services expanded, so now, in the transition to the second modernity, it is necessary to make a bold leap from the industry and service society to the knowledge and information society. This transition – argue authors such as Daniel Bell, Peter F. Drucker, Scott Lash/John Urry and Manuel Castells – will fundamentally change not only the world of work but the very concept of work itself. The most prominent feature of this new society will be the centrality of knowledge as an economic resource. Knowledge, not work, will become the source of social wealth; and 'knowledge workers' who have the capacity to translate specialized knowledge into profit-producing innovations (products, technological and organizational innovations, etc.) will become the privileged group in society.

The basic economic resource – the 'means of production' to use the economist's term – is no longer capital, nor natural resources (the economist's 'land'), nor 'labour'. *It is and will be knowledge.* The central wealth-creating activities will be neither the allocation of capital to productive uses nor 'labour' – the two poles of nineteenth- and twentieth-century economic theory, whether Classical, Marxist, Keynesian or Neo-Classical. Value is now created by 'productivity' and 'innovation', both applications of knowledge to work. The leading social groups of the knowledge society will be 'knowledge workers' – knowledge executives who know how to allocate knowledge to productive use; knowledge professionals; knowledge employees. Practically all these knowledge people will be employed in organizations. Yet unlike the employees under capitalism they own both the 'means of production' and the 'tools of production' – the former through their pension funds which are rapidly emerging in all developed countries as the only real owners, the latter because knowledge workers own their knowledge and can take it with them wherever they go. The *economic* challenge of the post-capitalist society will therefore be the productivity of knowledge work and knowledge worker.[20]

Many have objected that there is nothing new in this line of argument, since knowledge already played a central role in the industry and services era, perhaps in all epochs of work. Three answers can nevertheless be extracted from the different accounts.

1   *Science-dependent reflexive productivity.* The outstanding feature of knowledge work is the self-application of knowledge to knowledge as the main source of productivity. There is a circle between science-based technological innovations and the application of these technologies to produce new science-based generations of technologies and products, so that the productivity spiral of the knowledge society is not only kept going but accelerated.

2   *The trans-sectoral dynamic.* No new sector of production comes into being with the transition to the knowledge society. Rather, science-dependent productivity increases affect and change *all* sectors of production – agriculture, industry and services – and cancel the distinction between 'goods' and 'services'. In the end, talk of a 'postindustrial' or 'service' society becomes as mythical as the old distinction between a first, second and third sector becomes invalid.

3   *Despatialization of work and the indeterminism of information technology.* Those who try to explain the dynamic of the knowledge society with the assumptions and categories of the old paradigm of work fail to see its real revolutionary potential, which is that it enables different kinds of activity – production, management, application and distribution – to be directly linked up online. In the process, however, the location paradigm of industrial society breaks down and a new diversity of options compels decisions and requires standardization. Consequently, technological determinism is refuted by information technology. The knowledge society develops pluralistically out of itself, varying in a relationship of mutual dependence with the various norms and paths of development in different spheres and societies and against different cultural backgrounds. At the same time, in the knowledge society, distribution of and access to knowledge become a key element of new social inequalities and conflicts.

This is already beginning to emerge in the world market metropolises, in the form of social divisions. The expansion of global finance has created employment opportunities not only for highly skilled, and highly paid, specialists, but also for low-paid and unskilled labour. The system of brokers, investment bankers, data-processing experts, programmers, estate agents and insurance professionals can function only if there are a mass of people who tidy up, clean, maintain, supply and protect. A neo-feudal service society tied to a particular locality is a society that 'serves'. The ideal of service is being discovered by the very people who need it: the 'global players'.

Scenario 2: capitalism without work

The prophecy that the knowledge society will develop new creative sources of labour and productivity has not gone unchallenged. Chief among the sceptics is the venerable Club of Rome. According to its view of things, the historical assurance that the dismantling of the old full-employment society will be accompanied by the development of a new, science-based society fails to appreciate what is radically new in the information and communication technologies: namely, their capacity to increase productivity *without* work. There are already very rough indicators that this is so. In Germany, for instance, the amount of paid work per head of the population has been continually declining since 1955, so that only 60 per cent of the 1955 total of working hours is still performed today. At the same time, the average length of the working week fell from 48 hours in 1955 to 37.4 hours in 1996.[21]

Up to the mid-1970s, employment trends still followed the economic cycle. For example, the number of people out of work rose dramatically in the crisis years of 1967 and 1975, only to fall again subsequently below 300,000. Apart from these exceptional periods, full employment remained the rule. But then the oil crisis destroyed this shining world of the full employment society. Slight conjunctural fluctuations aside, the number of unemployed rose tenfold between 1970 and 1996.[22]

42

Thus, ever since the 1970s unemployment has been constantly rising and the amount of work per capita has been constantly falling. This conclusion, which is used to counter the optimistic view that information technology will bring full employment, suggests that although the knowledge society is opening up new fields of work, it is gradually easing itself away from the normal work society.

If it is true that technologically advanced capitalism reduces the number of well-paid and secure full-time jobs, then societies of the second modernity will have to choose between conflicting paths of development. Either there will be mass unemployment and society will split between those with and those without a job, with all the dangers this implies for democracy. Or else it will be seen as necessary to move away from the work society: that is, to redefine work and employment, to open ways to a new order covering not only the social and corporate organization of work, but the values, goals and normal biographies in society as a whole.

Jeremy Rifkin has shown that in the United States the proportion of factory workers in the economically active population fell over the past thirty years from 33 per cent to 17 per cent, even though there was a sharp rise in industrial output.[23] In ten years' time less than 12 per cent of America's working population will be employed in factories – and by the year 2020 the figure will be less than 2 per cent. Moreover, even in the classical service sectors where hopes are directed towards a new jobs miracle, automation and downsizing have long since begun. Those who boost the economy further will not only fail to overcome structural unemployment; they will actually reinforce it. For flourishing enterprises make their profits mainly through rationalization (and no one can be blamed for that in an economic system geared to profit). Why should they create jobs when machines can work much more efficiently than people?

In Rifkin's view, the industrial age put an end to slave labour, but the information age will do away with mass employment. The new technologies promise hugely increased production of goods and services in the twenty-first century, but only a fraction of the numbers employed today will be needed for it. Since virtual firms and factories almost empty of people are what the future holds in store, every person and every country must consider the question of how society, democracy, freedom and social security will be possible in the post-work society.

Scenario 3: the world market – the neoliberal jobs miracle

Black magic, is the answer that the world power of neoliberalism gives to this question. Just look at the United States! Look at Asia! Full-employment societies blossoming on all sides. Of course, such references to the tiger economies have become rather out-dated, now that they are one of the world's crisis regions. Radical political measures are accordingly prescribed as the royal road back to full employment: highly stable value of money, moderate wage increases and low strike rates, combined with a minimal state that does no more than provide a competitive social frame-work where individual citizens and companies bear much of the responsibility themselves. Strategies to bring back a welfare-state type of full employment (job-creation programmes, expansion of public services, etc.) are treated as the devil's work, supposedly because they would simply worsen the problem of unemployment after a brief respite. As far as the labour market is concerned, successful countries such as the United States, Norway, New Zealand, Portugal and the recently much-praised Netherlands offer markedly lower fiscal burdens and social contributions, a higher rate of investment, reduced wage-rates, hardly any strikes, and a high proportion of part-time work.

At least three strategic objections may be made against the foregoing line of argument.

1   Neoliberalism is culturally blind, both in its view of its own historical origins and in its naive belief in the universal validity of its 'laws'. It thereby reinforces the suspicion of imperialism that was already proving to be the flaw of mod-ernization policies in the 1960s. There is no patented world solution to unemployment.

2   The reduction of unemployment with the help of radical neoliberal medicine generates new and sharper problems. Societies such as the United States or Britain are proving

44

this before our very eyes. They have reduced the problem of unemployment and exchanged it for problems such as low wages, low productivity, low social security, growing income inequality and, especially in America, dramatically higher rates of imprisonment.

3   Is the so-called neoliberal way the only way of bringing down unemployment? The answer is: no. A glance at the Netherlands or Scandinavia shows that there too unemployment has been significantly reduced in a short period of time – not through application of the American model, but through active labour-market policies, part-time work, a radical cheapening of labour-power, and a range of economies. In each case this has involved collective agreements and thus what we might call the European neocorporatist path.

Another reason why the word 'globalization' makes people apprehensive is that it is often one-sidedly equated with the export of jobs. For example, Taiwanese workers may take a US microprocessor, insert it into a disc drive made in Singapore, put the whole thing inside plastic casing produced in China, and finally ship it to Europe to be sold there as an 'American' product. The problem lies much deeper, however, and the fear of global competition overlooks two things.

First, export-intensive sectors of the economy are dependent not only upon the site of direct workplace interaction, but also upon a wider regional economy that includes insurance representatives, financial advisers, employees in snack bars or fitness centres, dentists and others who offer their wares for sale locally. In this sense, globalization presupposes localization – a service society tied to the locality.

Second, products that can be produced and traded 'transnationally', sent here and there with unprecedented dedication, make up an ever-shrinking proportion of the world economy. Productivity is rising fast in sectors where the necessary information can be fairly easily standardized and programmed into a computer or robot. At the same time, demand is growing for a whole range of other activities that rely upon 'common sense' in dealing with customers – even if many of them are paid less because of their lower productivity.

Scenario 4: the fixed location of work – a globalization risk

The globalization optimists overlook another series of questions. If globalization has long been a fact – for example, in the dimension of finance markets – does this new basic situation have the same consequences, the same opportunities and risks, for both capital and labour? Does the global economy promote or generate a 'global labour market', in the sense that job-seekers are or may become as mobile as 'financial flows'? Can a globally oriented and organized labour movement ever take up position opposite a globally oriented and organized capital?

These questions must obviously be answered in the negative. Whereas capital can move across the globe in seconds via the electronic media, the mobility of working people is today – and will remain for the foreseeable future – severely limited by family and local ties, by institutions, laws and culture, by politics and the police, by protectionist movements and even hostility to foreigners. In international terms, it is by now a fast-shrinking phenomenon. In 1993 only some 1.5 per cent of the global labour force – roughly 80 million workers – were working outside their country of origin, and half of these were concentrated in Africa and the Middle East. In the European Union, where the free movement of labour between member-states is guaranteed by law, only 2 per cent of the national working populations were employed in another country of the EU. Contrary to the 'ship is full' rhetoric so prevalent among the public and in the foreign policy of states in the region, the number of immigrant workers in the major West European countries was lower at the end of the 1980s than it had been in 1975.

It may even be said that

> there is a historical tendency toward increasing interdependence of the labour force on a global scale, through three mechanisms: global employment in the multinational corporations and their associated cross-border networks; impacts of international trade on employment and labour conditions, both in the North and in the South; and effects of global competition and of the new mode of flexible management on each country's labour force.

46

Yet the fact remains: 'At its core, capital is global. As a rule, labour is local.' The dynamic of the knowledge society favours the concentration and globalization of capital, precisely because the decentralizing power of networks is brought into play, while 'there is at the same time differentiation of work, segmentation of workers, and disaggregation of labour on a global scale . . . Labour loses its collective identity, becomes increasingly individualized in its capacities, in its working conditions, and in its interests and projects.'[24]

The fixed location of labour means that working people are losers in the struggle to distribute the global risks of globalization. The Asian financial crisis and its consequences shed a bright light upon the previously darkened side of the *economic* world risk society. Not only do they provide a most striking example of organized irresponsibility; they have also made it clear that whole countries and groups of countries can become victims of global 'casino capitalism'. The Asian middle classes have been cut to the quick and are threatened in the very basis of their existence. Waves of bankruptcies and unemployment are shaking the region to a simply unimaginable degree.

From their own economic viewpoint, Western investors and commentators usually perceive the Asian crisis as a threat to the finance markets. But they thereby fail to recognize its true explosive potential. For the global dangers of economic globalization mainly threaten and attack the conditions of existence for local-national labour: the middle classes are impoverished, the poor become complete have-nots, and the economic and political elites lose their legitimacy. We may speak quite simply of a threatening implosion of the class and social order. Global financial risks also develop a 'socially explosive force',[25] which undermines state bureaucracies, calls the dominant neoliberal economic policies into question, and confuses the dividing-lines and power positions in national and inter-national politics. Suddenly the issue of 'responsible globalization' is being raised and debated throughout the world.

For this reason, it is no exaggeration to speak of an 'economic Chernobyl'. Indeed, just as ecological world risk society (Beck 1999) can be elucidated by reference to the 'anthropological shock' that the Chernobyl meltdown caused in Europe, the characteristics and the dynamic of economic world risk society in 1998 may be explained in terms of the social and political consequences of the Asian crisis.

This also applies to the emerging debate on new political options and institutions (regional and national protectionism, transnational insurance systems, global political tax institutions, and their democratic legitimation). This means that the appearance of non-political, neoliberal world-market fatalism is breaking down. World risk society is thus the opposite of a 'postmodern constellation'. It is a new kind of highly political, partly self-critical society, in which transnational dialogue, politics and democracy have a chance to develop on the basis of the politically explosive power of, among other things, the looming economic and ecological risks to the world.

Scenario 5: sustainable work – the ecological economic miracle

Once the limitations of Western-style growth were recognized, the search was on for an alternative, 'sustainable' model of development. The most commonly quoted definition of 'sustainability' comes from the report of the Brundtland Commission: 'Humanity has the ability to make development sustainable – to ensure that it meets the needs of the present without compromising the ability of future generations to meet their own needs. . . . sustainable development requires meeting the basic needs of all and extending to all the opportunity to fulfil their aspirations for a better life.'[26]

According to this definition, sustainable development is more than just protection of nature or caution about the eco-system. It also includes new models of social development and social transformation. Two central aspects of the concept that keep recurring in debate are economic growth and equality between countries, generations and, not least, the sexes.

Whereas technological advances raise productivity and reduce the importance of human labour, the point now – in the context of 'sustainable' economic activity and work – is to increase the productivity of nature and especially of energy. If the productivity of energy could be increased by a factor of four, it might permit a successful turn to 'sustainable development'. As a matter of fact, it is possible to derive from a barrel of oil, a kilowatt-hour of electricity or a tonne of soil, four times the existing levels of energy efficiency, as Ernst Ulrich von Weizsäcker has impressively shown in *Das Jahrhundert der Umwelt*.[27]

In a 'sustainable' economy, the main focus of work would shift from production to maintenance, repair and other services. These new 'sustainable' areas of work would be solar-intensive and time-intensive, but might also be both technologically advanced and to a large degree decentralized – a skill and activity profile geared to the use of modern information and communications technology for ecological economics and activity.

The centrepiece of this scenario is the idea of an ecological tax. According to this model, which would seem to rule itself out rather like the squaring of a circle, a tax on the use of nature is coupled with the cheapening of labour; the government lowers secondary wage-costs (employers' pension contributions, and so on) and compensates for this with a tax on consumption. This is supposed to solve two key problems at once: labour becomes cheaper and energy more expensive, resulting in more employment and more environmental protection!

Supporters of this approach see it as pointing towards a social-ecological miracle for work and the economy. The following points are made to illustrate this combined ecologization of work and employment.

- Every job lost through the shutdown of nuclear power stations brings five jobs into wind energy. For five years this sector has had a 100 per cent growth rate each year. This means growth at the right place in the economy. On any realistic medium-term calculation, moreover, electrical current derived from wind energy will be decidedly cheaper than electricity from a nuclear power station.
- By the year 2000, 1.1 million people in Germany will be employed in environmental protection (according to the Federal Environmental Bureau).
- The introduction of an energy and carbon emissions tax will bring 650,000 new jobs into the processing industry and the service sector (according to the Economic Research Institute).
- Transport changes over the next twenty-five years, through a

massive expansion of public systems, will create a million new jobs (according to the Transport Ministry of North Rhine-Westphalia).

- Technologies for the improvement of water efficiency will require 200,000 jobs in Germany (according to Berlin's Environmental Senate).
- A European Union study predicts 5 million new jobs in Europe over the next ten years as a result of the changeover to solar energy.

National or Europe-wide ecological taxes may be seen as, and be politically introduced as, part of an overall strategy of ecological conversion. This associates *government intervention* with the *mobilization of civil society* and *self-guiding control* of the economy. An example of government intervention is the legal regulation of market operations through the setting of pollution limits, as well as political objectives such as the switch from nuclear to solar energy, traffic restrictions, and so on. An element coming from civil society is a conscious change in consumption behaviour; the farewell to the car, for instance, is not only a question of costs and traffic planning, but a political decision about alternative lifestyles. This also includes expanded rights and duties of economic participation, and acceptance of the goals of 'sustainable' work and economic activity and of the need to test them out in experiments.

Scenario 6: global apartheid

In the past twenty years, the rate of female employment has risen worldwide from 36 per cent to 40 per cent. For the World Bank, women are among the winners of economic globalization. But this does not take account of the fact that women are especially affected by the worldwide *informalization* of employment relations – more part-time work, fluid boundaries between the formal and informal sectors, home-based work, a lack of legal regulation – which accompanies growth in both the old and new industrialized economies and the developing countries.

The Indian social scientist and ecologist Vandana Shiva speaks in this regard of a growing worldwide split between rich and poor, which is tantamount to 'global apartheid'. The key distinction she draws is between those who participate in the global economy and those whose basic conditions for life have been destroyed. Ecological globalization risks also find local expression. And the crises of ecology and justice form an inner unity: 'There can be no justice between the sexes in a world of ecological crises and global apartheid, if the social and political structures that protect the poor are dismantled because they "block" free trade or are considered "inefficient" or "extravagant" in the sense of the market logic of profit maximization.'[28]

In so far as capitalist successes based on information technology remove the shackles of human labour, reports of victories and bad tidings become two sides of the same coin. Both the profits of transnational corporations and the unemployment figures are on the rise in the welfare niche-societies of Western Europe. The same trend that means a roller-coaster for the economy is becoming a living nightmare for working people. They are no longer needed.

If this is related to the sectoral shift in Germany, it is easy to agree with the US economic theorist Michael E. Porter that German capitalism is losing the 'diamond' that gave it such a crucial international advantage.[29] For Porter, the diamond is an image in which a country's national economic base is combined with its cultural specificities and political objectives, which together underpin its position on the world market. Until well into the 1970s, Germany's 'Fordist diamond' was bound up with the joint productivity of the key automobile, chemicals, foodstuffs, engineering and electrical sectors. Their success rested in turn upon a unique set of historical, cultural and political conditions:

- the proprietary 'skilled worker' and a corresponding culture of training and lifestyle;
- mass demand in the home market for mass-produced goods;
- a matching local supply economy;
- strong trade unions and free collective bargaining that was also highly valued by politicians;
- a corporate culture geared to partnership between both sides of industry;
- a guiding political image of 'working citizens', which replaced

51

talk of class struggle with moderate negotiating practices and a commitment to democratic institutions.

While Germany's postwar economic miracle led to collective advancement that favoured acceptance of the democratic system, both the question of unemployment and the question of democracy are posed differently in the 'post-national constellation' in which the German model has been losing the ground beneath its feet. This is happening in connection with the emergence of a political image of a society beyond full employment.

> Uncertainties about how people can and want to lead their lives in the future have become much more acute. Around the end of the eighties, the bursting of 'traditional fetters' was celebrated in the name of individualization. Now the promise that people can take their fate into their own hands, regardless of origin and gender, is turning into a curse bound up with incessant social threats. Instead of setting off for the land of new opportunities, people are afraid that all previous gains will tomorrow vanish into thin air. Instead of the promised classless society, the old 'fine distinctions' (Bourdieu) are suddenly changing into a new kind of intense social polarization. Instead of an elevator effect for all layers in society, a revolving-door effect admits a few winners and casts out many losers.[30]

Some would even argue that, from the resulting breakdown, conflicts and legitimation problems, ecological and civil wars may ultimately arise in the Western democracies. The possibility must also be considered of various kinds of fundamentalism and xenophobic violence – sinister, ghastly developments that reinforce one another and draw out the catastrophic potential of the age.

In this neo-Spenglerism, a central role is often played by population trends. Since the world's poorest have the highest birth-rates, while the wealthiest bring fewer and fewer children into the world, equality could in the end come about only through worldwide migratory flows – which would lead to the strengthening of Fortress Europe and tendencies toward separation.

Scenario 7: the self-employed
– the freedom of insecurity

One of the most striking features of the second modernity is the paradoxically collective wish to live 'a life of one's own'. This individualized horizon of meaning has not fallen from the skies, nor has it taken root and grown as an individual hope in the hearts of all men and women. It represents a deep historical-cultural change, which was already observed and recorded in earlier epochs, especially the nineteenth century and the first half of the twentieth, but which acquired new expressions and momentum in the European welfare states of the postwar period. Especially since the 1970s, the expansion of education – whose effects can hardly be overestimated – as well as the general enrichment and the internalization of basic political and social rights (which were always geared to individuals), have resulted in a kind of fully comprehensive individualization. This has broken people away from the certainties of their original milieu and made them authors of their own lives – with all the turbulent consequences for political organization and voting behaviour, family and marriage, intimacy and sexuality.

Ever since the 1980s, but at accelerating speed in the 1990s, this individualization of lifeworlds has been compounded, overlaid and counteracted by an individualization of work. The normal work situation – normal both for individual lives and for company policy – has begun to break down, and a political economy of insecurity and differentiation has developed in place of an economy of state-guaranteed social security. This process of dissolution affects basic oppositions that used to be taken for granted and to bind individuals and institutions together in the European societies of the first modernity: labour and capital, firm and market, self-employed and employee, housework and job, work on one's own account and heteronomous wage-labour. Paid employment is being 'chopped up' both contractually and temporally, and with it the unifying time structure of social life in family, neighbourhood and community. The result is a new space for action and decision, which is in principle double-edged. On the one hand, there is new freedom to shape and coordinate one's 'own' work and one's 'own' life; but on the other hand, new trapdoors can lead to exclusion, and the risks are shifted from the state and the economy on to the shoulders of individuals. Both aspects are based on the new precariousness of work; the opportunities come with risks attached.

The 'individualization of work' must now be briefly considered in its two opposing scenarios, of hope and disintegration.

Various labels evoking deviance, discrimination or subcultural profusion are currently employed to characterize the individualized forms of work and employment. Typically, there are no systematic assessments but only estimates of their scale – indeed, it is even questionable whether the general categories used in official statistics can still grasp the orchid-like diversity that is becoming the norm.

'Outsourcing', one of these labels, should be understood as meaning 'hiving off', as the possibility for companies to engage in 'cooperation' across open frontiers. Book-keeping operations may be relocated to another country, as may telephone switchboards or filing systems, and these parts of the business also sell their services on the open market. In this way, the market (which used to be seen as conceptually opposed to the company) is brought inside the company, as it were, so that the old rigid boundaries between inside and outside crumble and fall away.

This is also true of 'franchising' – which means that company names, products and brand-names are put up for sale. The 'franchise-holder' does not fall under an Either-Or typical of the first modernity – either employer or employee – but is a new kind of Both-And. 'The modern self-employed are their own bosses, the more successful, the more they are ideal collaborators', writes Peter Fischer.[31]

In a number of ways, these seemingly independent operators are 'self-employers': they embody a cross between employer and day-labourer, self-exploiter and boss on their own account, whose transcontinental labour (in direct bondage to their client) is socially at once highly sensitive, highly cooperative and isolated. They work on their own life as if it were a work of art, yet have to obey the dictates of competition and global corporate power. The spreading of activities and sources of income reduces the risk. But it would not do to offer oneself as a jack of all trades: that would just expose one to all the tricks of the competition, as well as endangering one's own market niche and the stocks of competence and trust built up through collaboration with colleagues and clients. In other words, an art of muddling through is upon us.

Muddling through describes a new society of people working on their own account. These one-man or one-woman businesses have only a limited amount in common with traditional notions of entrepreneurship. Besides, their objective is much more likely to be the moulding of a life of one's own than conquest of the world market. If it is successful, so much the better. But in case of doubt, a badly paid service job may also be accepted as a meaningful part of an individual's history of paid work. Such a history would then, in the nature of things, be full of breaks and contradictions; education would be interrupted and resumed, McJobs would often rank equally with starting up in a business of one's own, and everything would be woven together into a quite individual web of activities and employment situations. One thing, however, is common to all these life-constructions: they lie outside the classical employee's biography, outside union agreements and statutory salary scales, outside collective bargaining and home mortgage contracts.[32]

And they are the basis for a precarious new culture of independence: 'business men and women in their own affairs'.

Scenario 8: individualization of work – disintegration of society

Linda's new working life is not without its drawbacks. Chief among them is a constant cloud of anxiety about finding the next job. In some ways Linda feels isolated and vulnerable. Fearful of the stigma of having been laid off, for example, she doesn't want her last name to appear in this article. But the freedom of being her own boss makes up for the insecurity. Linda gets to build her schedule around her son's. She gets to find her own assignments. And she gets to be a pioneer of the new work force.[33]

We are eyewitnesses to a historic turnaround in the work society. The first modernity was characterized by the standardization of work; the second modernity is marked by the opposite principle of the individualization of work. The new potential of information technology – and we are certainly only at the beginning of an ongoing revolution – plays an important role by making possible both the decentralization of work tasks and their real-time coordination in interactive networks, whether across continents or across corridors. The gradual accompanying *inner globalization* of what used to be 'internal to the company' – that is, of an organization of work tied to the locality – leads to an insidious implosion of basic distinctions and certainties. Here the revolution is signalled by a new set of enigmatic terms developed in the social laboratory of management, which sound all the more enigmatic when directly incorporated as 'foreign terms' into other languages: lean production, subcontracting, outsourcing, offshoring, downsizing, customizing, to name but a few.

The most striking feature of this trend is that it is developing fastest in relation to precarious and hybrid forms of employment. If it has already been true for Southern European countries such as Italy or Spain that informal work makes up a large part of the total (more than 30 per cent), it now also holds for the countries at the forefront of neoliberal reform policies: Britain and the United States. The United Kingdom, which once pioneered the standardization of work, is now pioneering its individualization. Already at the beginning of the 1990s, nearly 40 per cent of work there did not conform to standard specifications (most of it in the form of part-time work, of which 85 per cent was done by women). The process of destandardization has since accelerated still more.[34]

Both the OECD and the International Labour Organization report that part-time work has spread rapidly in the 1980s and 1990s in practically all the early-industrialized countries, and stood at between 30 per cent and 40 per cent of the total at the beginning of the 1990s. (The category 'flexible work' comprises part-time work, inconsequential and temporary employment, spurious forms of self-employment, and so on.)

When the individualization of life and the individualization of work coincide and reinforce each other, society is in danger of falling apart. 'Under the conditions of the network society, capital is globally coordinated, labour is individualized. The struggle between diverse capitalists and miscellaneous working classes is subsumed into the more fundamental opposition between the bare logic of capital flows and the cultural values of human experience.'[35]

Perhaps this thoroughly capitalized kind of working life may best be represented by a satirical sketch.

A cautionary satire

The worst case in the social market economy is personal care: it does too little, makes too little profit, for others. Capitalism is youthful and hates crutches, prostheses and wheelchairs. An ill person is an anti-capitalist and a nuisance to the company. A very ill person is a terrorist and a menace to jobs. A very very ill person abuses the social safety-net and the employer's goodwill. To continue paying wages during sickness leads to socialism. It has to stop! . . .

Since we became younger, we have been more productive. Hardly a single one of us does not have the strength for five McJobs! Everyone delivers five newspapers at five in the morning, then takes five dogs for a walk, then fries burgers for half the day, then helps out for the other half in a health-food shop or a dry-cleaner's, and finally goes to work in a bar for the evening. The service society does indeed keep us all youthful. Anyone who is not flexible and does not have four legs has simply not understood the dollar sign of the age. Your own fault, old man! We are young and globalization is open to us – so the slogan goes. Yes, that only gives you grey hairs, and solidarity is like falling hair and bad breath rolled into one. Everyone brushes their teeth in the morning with Elmex, and uses Aronal at night to rub the day's catch from their fangs.

Since we became younger, we have . . . democracy, to which we say yes, yes, and Communism, to which we angrily say no, no. Meanwhile we have all grown closer to one another, networked and webbed, cabled and cordlessed. More and more jobless people pick up their wages and income in a quick and easy manner via automated City-Banking. More and more homeless people and refugees take the liberty of writing visa cards for themselves from all corners of the world. More and more fellow-citizens go to the stock exchange or invest their money in shares or whatever. Only those who do not yet own a mobile are left with only their own hands to get themselves off.[36]

Scenario 9: the multi-activity society

All the preceding future scenarios remain in one way or another – in hope or in fear – trapped in a conception of paid work as central to society, personal biographies and politics. If it is assumed, however, that the amount of paid employment is shrinking, then a change of paradigm or framework is required. The question becomes which guiding idea, or ideas, will appear in place of the fixation on paid work. Or, to put it in another way, to what extent can alternative visions beyond the full-employment society already be glimpsed in people's living and working conditions and the projects they make for themselves?

I would now like to touch upon two such scenarios pointing beyond the work society that are already a focus of heated public debate: namely, the multi-activity society and – in the next section – the leisure society. A third sketch, in which Europe is envisaged as a transnational civil society, will be considered in detail in the concluding two chapters.

In the transition from the work society to the multi-activity society, a new answer is given to the question: what is work? The concept of an 'activity society' does, it is true, include a reference to paid work, but only as one form of activity alongside others such as family work, parental work, work for oneself, voluntary work or political activity. This reminds us that people's everyday lives and work are stretched on the Procrustean bed of *plural activities* – a self-evident fact that is usually obscured in the perspective of a society centred upon paid employment.

Paid work, writes Elisabeth Beck-Gernsheim, has always been a 'one-and-a-half person occupation'.[37] The so-called normal work situation was tailored to men who had a wife in the background to take care of 'everything else' – children, meals, washing and cleaning, emotional equilibrium, everyday therapy, and so on. But the feminist movement and associated researchers, in particular, have always vehemently opposed the notion that a paid job is the only kind of work that has any social significance.

Nevertheless, such an opening out of the monogamous work society towards a multi-activity society requires a lot of conditions to be fulfilled. Something has to change not only in office workplaces, or in law and politics, but above all in people's (men's) heads. The idea that social identity and status depend only upon a person's occupation and career must be taken apart and abandoned, so that social esteem and security are really uncoupled from paid employment. This presupposes not only a readiness and willingness to develop varied sources of income – which, in the case of income from capital, can be rather a cynical piece of advice for the poor and homeless – but also the construction of a system of basic security that has at its core the right to breaks in lifetime employment.

Talk of a 'multi-activity society' has a double meaning that is worth noting. On the one hand, companies might take it to imply greater worker flexibility for their own ends. If, for example, a number of firms agreed to create a common pool of employees that they could share around according to circumstances, this would give the workers a 'multiple contract' but no new autonomy over their lives. Instead, they would be more than ever at the mercy of fluctuating demand and the use of their abilities would be controlled by more than one company.[38] Significantly enough, this class of 'permanent temporaries' is increasing especially fast in areas of employment that combine high prestige and good pay with high technological skills. They often do the same work as the regular staff, but have less social insurance, fewer paid holidays, and so on. In the high-tech sectors where most of these jobs arise, it is precisely the centralized firms such as Microsoft, AT&T or Boeing which make use of this highly flexible form of employment. In 1986 there were a total of 800,000 employees in this category, who continuously switched between different firms. By 1997 they already accounted for 2.5 million (or 2 per cent of the labour force) in the United States – and the trend was still upward. This kind of 'multi-employment contract' ultimately forces people to subordinate more and more of their outside activities to the pressures of economics.

On the other hand, an organization of 'young managers' in France has suggested a kind of employment contract that would make the 'reappropriation of time' a possibility for each individual. Control over one's own time, they argue, will be 'the true wealth in the years ahead and may mean that people are no longer held down by economic constraints. . . . If each citizen is to be given the capacity to control their own time-capital, they must be freed from the necessity of tying it up to make a living – of sacrificing their life to earn a living.'[39] The concrete objective is that a kind of constant bargaining would reduce and spread the agreed amount of working time, so that this would become both undifferentiated (a total to be worked over one or several years) and individual (the total for a particular week or month). Such a contract would enable each and every person to draw up a time plan of their own choosing. The company would guarantee their income and status, and above all their right to an uninterrupted income for a discontinuous working life decided by themselves. This type of multi-employment contract assumes that, today and in the future, the economically active population is entitled to a 'freely chosen time-framework'. It allows companies greater flexibility in their use of labour, but it also gives employees a new kind of time-autonomy and a new relationship to paid labour, because it recognizes and secures fields of activity outside work and affirms the cultural value of shaping 'one's own life'. In this way, the jobs society might really be replaced by a society of multiple activities and multiply active people.

André Gorz argues that a political reform is essential for the survival – or better, the restoration – of a society in which both individuals and companies can develop through the use of new informational technologies, and in which the insecure, discontinuous and radically changing modes of paid labour lead not to breakdown but to new forms of sociability and coexistence.[40] Keynes, for his part, already thought that we would have to spread the butter thin to distribute the work that still needed to be done; and that three-hour shifts and fifteen-hour weeks would keep things going for a while, because they would be enough to quiet the old Adam in us.

New ways of distributing work – shorter hours without full retention of pay, flexibilization, part-time work, abolition of over-time – are becoming necessary for the following reasons. First, they are the answer to the huge advances in productivity that are reducing the amount of work. Second, they may be able to alleviate or prevent new class divisions between the some with too much work and the others with none. Only when every man and woman has one foot in paid employment, and perhaps the other in civil labour, will it be possible to avoid a situation where the 'third sector' (Jeremy Rifkin) becomes a ghetto of the poor. Third, men also respond to women's growing inclination for employment by drastically cutting their own working time. Just as women are leaving the private labour of child-rearing in favour of paid employment, so must men, for the sake of private labour with children, deliberately interrupt their job history and not cling fanatically to paid employment.

'We are burning violins as fuel for steam engines', warns Friethjof Bergmann. That is: the most valuable human and natural resources are being squandered to keep obsolete employment machinery in service. Bergmann advocates a modified form of 'full employment', since in his view work is never-ending and it is a misunderstanding to think that we will ever run out of it. What he means, however, is not paid work but the wealth of creative and socially necessary activities.

Bergmann's vision is that everyone will spend two days a week at a paid job, two days working for themselves, and two days 'doing what they really really want to do'. This might be things of substance, which perhaps even lead to new paid activities. But in any event, he wants to mine 'the gold in people's heads', as much among the homeless and unemployed as among those with a demanding job.[41]

In the future model of a multi-activity society, then, it is not Either-Or but Both-And – alternation between a paid job, work in the family, civil labour, etc. – which will become increasingly significant. Does this mean that the contradictory image associated with women's work, torn between socially separate activities, will become the norm?

Scenario 10: the free-time society

In *The Gay Science*, Friedrich Nietzsche already ironically depicted how play and leisure, the Other of work, are imbued with work and its measures of value.

> More and more, work enlists all good conscience on its side; the desire for joy already calls itself a 'need to recuperate' and is beginning to be ashamed of itself. 'One owes it to one's health' – that is what people say when they are caught on an excursion into the country. Soon we may well reach the point where people can no longer give in to the desire for a *vita contemplativa* (that is, taking a walk with ideas and friends) without self-contempt and a bad conscience.[42]

The opposite of the work society is thus seen as the leisure or free-time society. There is a real danger that, in the highly developed West, a new class division will emerge between the active and the passive. People evicted from the labour process will be increasingly 'degraded' by the culture industries into 'entertainment patients totally in need of care' (Guggenberger). It is therefore important, as we approach the twenty-first century, that the leisure society which appears alongside the work society should no longer just be a matter of stopgap occupational therapy, but should rediscover and develop 'the art of squandering time' and 'the cultivation of the indirect'.[43]

One would certainly have thought that the concept of leisure, of *homo ludens*, should support an antithesis to the work society. Is it not true that play is everywhere finding a place for itself again? Wherever one looks, the global finance markets have brought 'casino capitalism' into being and lotteries stir millions of people; while sport, the most important thing in the world, continues to bind people's national aggressive energies and repeatedly explodes in spectacular mass violence. Does not play acquire a new everyday quality with the spread of the information industries, so that it actually conquers spaces in the world of work?

What is decisive in leisure and play is that things are done for their own sake. Traditionally, the concept of play refers to that which is dissociated from efficiency and success, cancelling purposive rationality and occurring for the pure pleasure of it. But it is also true that kids today get the hang of computers by playing computer games. Are they freely shaping themselves in the act of play, or are they potential employees of the computer and entertainment industries who put hard work even into play? The autism of computer games would seem to point to the latter.

Furthermore, leisure and play are unthinkable without work (or anyway without social activity). They are like the whipped milk and powdered chocolate that still require everyday coffee to make a cappuccino. In the absence of activity, compulsory leisure might easily become a hell on earth.

A summary

What happens when the work society runs out of work? To Hannah Arendt's well-known question, even radical sketches of the future ultimately give the paradoxical answer: work – not paid work, but work for a smile (domestic work, parental work, voluntary work, etc.). Every sketch that tries to cross the bridge to the other side of the work society maintains that there is no going beyond it. Everything is work, or else it is nothing.

This value imperialism in modern Europe's perception of itself may be explained by the chasm of irresponsibility that seems to open up with the end of paid work. Along which coordinates can people's lives be structured if there is no longer the discipline of a paid job? Is its loss not the root of all evil: drug addiction, crime, social disintegration? How can people's basic existence and social status be assured if these no longer rest upon performance at work? Which ideas of justice, or even of social inequality, can serve as the measure of people's lives, if society no longer thinks of itself as 'hard-working' or 'industrious'? What does the state mean if one of its most important sources of tax revenue – paid employment – dries up? How is democracy possible if it is not based upon participation in paid employment? How will people's social identity be determined, if they no longer have to tell themselves and others that 'what they do in life' is one of the standard occupations? What would be the meaning of governance, order, freedom – or even of society itself?

Visions that work will progressively disappear as the social norm rebound off the faith that most people still have in job miracles and in themselves as citizens of the work society. Having lost their faith in God, they believe instead in the godlike powers of work to provide everything sacred to them: prosperity, social position, personality, meaning in life, democracy, political cohesion. Just name any value of modernity, and I will show that it assumes the very thing about which it is silent: participation in paid work.

A critique of the future work scenarios

One way or another, the ten scenarios listed in Table 1 play an important role in this book. In varying degrees, however, their leap into the future always lands too short, still within the magic circle of the work society – and they also appear inadequate for a number of other major reasons.

Feminization of work

All scenarios in which multiple activity and multiple tracks replace 'monogamous work' (Peter Gross) easily end up in a zero-sum game of gender-divided labour. They make a virtue out of necessity by elevating shadow activities – housework, parental work, self-employed work, voluntary work – into the centre and source of meaning beyond the work society.

The road to hell is often paved with good intentions. What is here pictured as the society of the future may accordingly be identified and criticized as precarious *feminization* of the world of work. It is true that men who have to work only for a living arouse pity; they lack something important that comes from parental labour, work on their own account, and so on. At the same time, however, it makes little sense to redistribute scarcity by arguing that the precarious, discontinuous and contradictory aspects of female labour and the female life-world should also apply to men – or at least not if the ideal of women's equality through integration into standard work is simply reversed as men's integration into non-standard female work.

Does this not mean that everyone, men included, is caught in the 'patriarchal trap' deployed through the symbolic revaluation of domestic labour and self-employment? The personal may in a certain sense be political. But not only does such a gender equalization of insecurity conceal collective decline; it once more buries political society in the collective whirlpool of private disputes.

The rhetoric of 'full employment'

Many scenarios of a dual or multi-activity society boil down to a verbal trick. For they retain the grand promise of 'full employment', while actually turning it into its opposite: heteronomous paid work is supposed to be replaced by autonomous unpaid work.

The odour of the white lie soon attaches to fine talk about 'self-active civil society'. For what it actually means is no protection against dismissal at work; no union-negotiated job contracts; more responsibility for one's own security in sickness and old age. The 'self-active society' is then nothing more than maximum savings for public services and the private sector.

Ecological critique

It also needs to be asked whether the various models of the future seriously address and answer the ecological critique in relation to paid employment.[44] All work produces not only consumption of desired goods but also waste.[45] Paid work is itself rendered alien by its 'dual-purpose structure'. The workers' own interest in income, job security and status, which are abstract vis-à-vis the concrete goals of work, can be pursued only if the content of the work and its consequences for others are left out of account, in the sense of being 'instrumentalized' and tailored to the workers' own economic interests. For example, someone who solves a work problem under these conditions makes himself or herself redundant.[46] Ecologically speaking, there is ground for scepticism about whether, for example, a redistribution of such work would bring any improvement, since only a focus on the nature-destroying aspect of work could change the foundations of the work society in a meaningful direction that was up to the tasks of the future. In other words, the destructive force of work is not annulled if it simply becomes informal, dual, plural, unpaid, self-motivated, or whatever.

The question of the inclusive society

All suggested solutions to unemployment must ultimately face the test of whether they really help the ones they are supposed to help: the poor and needy who are threatened with exclusion. In the talk of a free-time or leisure society, for example, it may be that this applies to the German welfare niche but even there only to the diminishing circle of well-endowed permanent employees, not to the mass of people without job security. In the end, the crucial question to be asked is who is on board, who not on board – as Ralf Dahrendorf puts it. What will be done to ensure that everyone has the opportunities offered by this society? What must happen politically to ensure that everyone doing something outside the classical careers – whether on a short-term contract without job security or without any kind of contract – should nevertheless remain or become a full citizen? How can the basic right to participate in the basic rights of modernity be reaffirmed in a context of deregulation and fraying of the work society?

5

The Risk Regime

How the Work Society is Becoming Risk Society

Public debates are always dominated by the same crises, the same explanations, the same proposed solutions. Full employment is said to be possible if the course is set for economic growth: which means to lower wage costs, reduce unemployment benefit and income support, decrease taxes, create more investment incentives, cut down on bureaucratic regulation, improve education and training, provide risk capital, subsidize cheap-rate jobs. If it is true that a high level of standardization is the prerequisite for automation, then it will soon be possible to churn out this whole line of argument with computerized voices. And yet, it stands or falls with a premise that needs to be systematically questioned.

Often it is simply taken for granted that the waves of rationalization will lead to drastic changes in, but not of, the system of paid work; that there will be continuity in its basic categories and ideas (company, job, occupation, wage-labour, economic growth, opposition between capital and labour, and so on). Such a point of view denies that there has been or will be any constitutional change in the employment system as a result of the current or forthcoming processes of modernization, not only in information technology but also in the social and legal framework. By contrast, the paradigm of a second modernity has just such a systemic change at its centre.

In order to identify, investigate and conceptualize this systemic change of the jobs society, there has to be a change in our categories and our frame of reference. Attention must be redirected and sharply focused on that which is new. An attempt must now be made to introduce such a category-change against the background of the ten foregoing scenarios of the future of work, and to fill this in with data, dilemmas and political implications.

The Fordist regime

In the academic and wider public debate about changing structures of work, such keywords as 'post-industrialism', 'post-Taylorism', 'post-Fordism' or 'neo-Fordism' usually hold the stage. But for our purposes, we need to consider this debate only as a backdrop to the theory and sociology of work in the second modernity. The first key category, borrowed from Michel Aglietta, is that of regimes of accumulation internally connected to the dominant mode of regulation.[47] Regimes of accumulation denote periods of economic growth in terms of a fundamental correspondence between what is produced and what is consumed. The 'Fordist regime', for instance, rests upon the fact that the principle of mass standardization applies to both production and consumption. Labour and production are geared to large model runs of cars, refrigerators, washing-machines and the like, which allow rapid increases in productivity and profits and, via rising wages, also in mass consumption. This form of production, work and consumption created a society in which people's lives were as highly standardized as the sheet steel from which the cars were welded together.

> Pia Hinz's mother had a married life that was synchronized by the car factory. In the morning, on the early shift, Christel Hinz and her husband drove together to the factory car park and walked together through the tunnel; in the afternoon they went together back to the car park. On the late shift, it was the same, only later. Saturday and Sunday were free, and the family went to the Baltic coast. 'It was nicely organized' – the same finishing time for everyone, so the same rest time for everyone. If the lines stopped for half an hour, her husband looked by from the other hall. He squatted down in a rest area and Christel Hinz boiled some coffee.[48]

Nevertheless, the Fordist growth regime, consisting in mass production, mass labour and mass consumption, did not only mean fixed times for holidays and other activities that underpinned and standardized life together in family, neighbourhood and community. It was also shaped and reinforced by a 'mode of regulation', which supported the growth regime culturally, politically and legally. This involved a wide range of strategies, actors and conditions which tied company management, banks, trade unions and political parties, as well as governments, to a relatively uniform philosophy of growth and a corresponding set of measures that held out a promise of success. The cultural-political targets of these measures were citizens in full-time employment, who had expectations of rising living standards and job security, while the main recipes were workforce participation, free collective bargaining, strong trade unions, government intervention and Keynesian macro-policies. Since conjunctural downturns and rising unemployment were seen as caused by weak demand, the state was not supposed to stint on public expenditure, and employers were also urged to increase wages as a means of pushing up internal demand. The basic rule of Keynesianism was that rising demand would result in corporate investment and new jobs. Thus, under the conditions of Fordism, institutionalized expectations of constant economic growth, rising consumption, public affluence and social security constituted the 'social cement' of the regime.

This mode of regulation, which stamped and held together a whole era, permitted and indeed compelled different paths to be taken in different countries. Each national economy, whether the United States, Japan, France, Germany, Sweden or Britain, found its own way to Fordism. The history of a nation, its cultural-political peculiarities and its special place in the world market are bound up with national-cultural regimes of growth.

The risk regime

Even at the risk of oversimplification, I would like to propose the following distinction. The ongoing debate on the rise and fall of Fordist mass production, mass consumption and standardized full employment, as well as the corresponding picture of a standardized society and the political formula of Keynesianism, belong to the paradigm of the first modernity. In the second modernity, however, the risk regime prevails in every field: economy, society, polity. Here the appropriate distinction is therefore not between an industrial and post-industrial or Fordist and post-Fordist economy, but between the securities, certainties and clearly defined boundaries of the first modernity, and the insecurities, uncertainties and loss of boundaries in the second modernity.

It is also useful to distinguish between the cognitive insecurity that results from the unsafe judgements and lack of contours typical of transitional societies, and the (relatively) safe judgement that future society will be characterized by the risk regime. To speak of a 'risk regime' does not mean to have a transitional phenomenon before one's eyes. Rather, it refers to the foreseeable and conceptually clear principle of blurring or fuzziness which marks the picture of work, society and politics in the second modernity – even if the social structures or the individual, social and political responses associated with it cannot yet be truly foreseen, let alone detected.

In other words, the specificity of the risk regime is that it firmly rules out, beyond a transition period, any eventual recovery of the old certainties of standardized work, standard life histories, an old-style welfare state, national economic and labour policies. Rather, the concept of a risk regime refers to a key principle of the second modernity, whose 'logic' leads to new forms and images of economy and work, society and politics. Whereas the Fordist regime brought about the standardization of work, the risk regime involves an individualization of work. Whereas Fordism took no account of damage to the environment, the risk regime makes central the question of how capital and labour handle both the 'goods' and the 'bads' of prosperity.

The society corresponding to Fordism was standardized. But with the risk regime, people are expected to make their own life-plans, to be mobile and to provide for themselves in various ways. The new centre is becoming the precarious centre. Poverty is being 'dynamized': that is, cut up and distributed across life-sections. It is becoming a 'normal' – less and less often just a temporary – experience at the centre of society. Whereas Fordism and political Keynesianism presupposed the boundaries of the national state, and thus the standpoint and tax-raising potential of national politics and society, this orderly framework is superseded in the risk regime by a compulsion to relocate and prevail on the world market and in world society.

The concepts of risk and risk regime have a shimmering ambivalence. At one extreme, risk may be understood as an activation principle that is the glory of human civilization. 'Dancing on the edge of the volcano is the finest metaphor I know for risk. And finding the courage to risk is the most wonderful motive of all for dancing' (Maurice Béjart). But at the opposite extreme, risk means a creeping or galloping threat to human civilization and civil spirit, a catastrophic possibility that progress will swing round into barbarism. Here it activates, rather, a principle of precautions and moratoria. If a metaphor is desired, it might be that world risk society balances precariously out of reach of the (private) insurance which the first modernity erected to control the unpredictable consequences of decisions (Beck 1999). It is economics – not social or ecological movements and their critique of technology – whose verdict 'uninsured/uninsurable' blocks uncontrollable consequences and dangers of old and new technologies. This is true of nuclear energy/atomic power stations, which are insured only by the state, and even then to a degree quite inadequate for their destructive potential. But it is also true of biotechnology and human genetics, where the consequences are hidden in a cloud of scientifically produced uncertainty and insurance issues have so far not really been raised. Finally, there are publicly perceived risks that do politicize people, because they throw up the question of responsibility precisely where – under the prevailing rules of attribution in ethics, law and science – it is difficult or impossible to answer.

Such ambivalences of the risk regime may now help us to distinguish two paths for society beyond full employment – paths which, at least somewhere below the surface, give rise to political controversy. On the one hand, loss of the security associated with the Fordist system of standardized work is welcomed and politically accelerated as if it were a natural process. This paradoxical erosion of politics and society by politics and society, which I described above as the Brazilianization of the West, will be further analysed in the following sections. It is a question of side-effects of the American way, which has become the model for modernization in all parts of the world since the end of the East-West conflict.

On the other hand, the dominance of the risk regime poses the question of how loss of security can be converted into a blossoming of social creativity; how security and political freedom can be brought into harmony with each other beyond the fully comprehensive society. This concrete utopia of a political civil society may be the European road to the second modernity, spelling out anew the original idea of politics and democracy.

Both variants of development also point to the basic feature of the new diversity of work in the second modernity: namely, the growing multiplicity of answers and arrangements at a corporate, individual, social and political level. The actually emerging work profiles thus turn out to be the exact opposite of the quasi-naturalistic vision of a post-industrial service society ultimately based upon American ethnocentrism.

The risk regime entails that the future of work will involve more than one direction of development, within and across a number of different dimensions. The idea that a single dynamic – for example, digitalization or flexibilization of production – is capable of transforming the global economy in a single direction and towards a single goal belongs to the long-overrun conceptual world of the first modernity. Risk regime thus means compulsion to choose. It means individualization and pluralization – though against a backdrop of fabricated insecurities and uncertainties.

Dimensions of the risk regime: globalization, ecologization, digitalization, individualization and politicization of work

Risk regimes are networked regimes cutting across and through sectors and disciplines which pose the question of society anew. This is so because

> developments which at first sight seem 'remote from the labour market' will perhaps be of far greater significance for the future of work than are the long-predictable demographic faults or the equally

predictable crises of antiquated industries. Ecological disasters, for example, may suddenly change the framework in which whole national economies operate. Similarly momentous consequences may result from new safety thresholds and causes of pollution, as well as from changes in values, structural changes in social and cultural milieux, changes in the gender and family division of labour, or abrupt shifts in the global constellations of political power. The growing importance of such aspects – which, though 'remote from the labour market', baffle all economic *ceteris paribus* restrictions – has been accepted in recent discussions of the future of economic policy, all the more readily in that planning and risk-management strategies built upon standardized economic criteria continue to be perfected but can hardly provide any longer the hoped-for economic security.[49]

The risk regime – that is, the political economy of insecurity, uncertainty and loss of boundaries – may be analysed under the headings of globalization, ecologization, digitalization, individualization and politicization of work.[50]

Globalization

Whereas, in the Fordist regime, work and production are always tied to a locality, the risk regime sets off a social despatialization of work and production, and with it a dialectic of globalization and localization, which are still not at all predictable in their consequences. A kind of 'inner globalization' comes about, an 'inner mobility' of locally situated and networked producing 'companies'. The adjective 'virtual' has sometimes been used to describe this – as in virtual companies, virtual products, virtual work and cooperation. But, of course, 'virtual' should be understood not in the sense of 'fictitious' but in that of a new kind of translocal organization of production and work. A globalization risk is expressed not only in the unpredictable consequences of this diffuse (at once localized and globalized) mode of work, but also, among other things, in the fact that the risks of transnational capital flows predictably affect labour that is culturally tied to the locality and threaten the foundations of society and the state – as millions of new poor and unemployed people well know in Indonesia and other South-East Asian countries. Nor is it possible to insure oneself (either publicly or privately) against these economic risks of globalization.

73

Ecologization

When technological or ecological risks are publicly depicted in the risk-sensitive West, markets collapse, capital is devalued, experts and professional associations lose face and find themselves in the dock. This means that ecological risks are converted into capital risks, as well as into labour-market and occupational risks. At the same time, they trigger a redistribution of market changes for capital and labour. New occupational profiles, jobs, production sectors, product and service chains come into being and change risk definitions into new markets – from garbage sorters and landscape planners, through best-selling exports of environmental technology, to more or less 'green' foodstuffs, building materials, furniture and other accoutrements of daily life.

Ecologization and globalization mutually determine and intensify each other. In the past two decades, the ideology of a free world market has spread across the globe, with the result that environmental destruction has increased by roughly as much in the shadow of victorious neoliberalism as it did in the Soviet planned economy during the time of the Cold War. Against the background of free trade zones such as those created under GATT or NAFTA, consumption in the wealthiest countries has spun practically out of control, increasing sixfold in less than twenty-five years, according to UN figures. In other words, the richest 20 per cent of humanity consume roughly six times more food, energy, water, transport, oil and minerals than their parents used to do.

Digitalization

This also compels, and indeed facilitates, both globalization and individualization. The emerging global economy should not be confused with the 'world-system' of which Fernand Braudel and Immanuel Wallerstein speak. Global digitalization and networking are aimed at an economy that will have the capacity to operate as a unit in real time right across the planet. Digitalization should really be seen as the spread of a new kind of literacy: those who do not master computer language will be excluded from the circle of social communication. The 'grammar' of digital technology is not, however, the only element shaping people's view of the world; others are the scale and objectives of the flexibilization, virtualization and rationalization of work. A new type of 'high-tech' nomadic worker is appearing on the scene – or perhaps it would be more correct to speak of networked nomadic workers, capable, as it were, of being both here and there at the same time, of overcoming the gravity of space. They are no longer subject to an Either-Or, but to a Both-And. They are simultaneously at work and at home, isolated yet working with and for others – in the distanceless space beyond frontiers and continents, but also concretely networked in the here and now.

Individualization

This is perhaps the key result of the flexibilization of work. Three aspects are involved in it. A lifeworld process of detraditionalization means that the standard biography becomes an elective or do-it-yourself biography, a risk biography. Work is 'chopped up' by time and contract. And there is also an individualization of consumption: that is, individualized products and markets emerge.

Politicization

Here it is necessary to distinguish between two viewpoints and lines of development. On the one hand, there is a *subpoliticization* of economy and work. This results from the fact that globalization, ecologization, digitalization and individualization call into question the basic certainties of (Fordist-standardized) work and life; but also from the fact that no one can insist any longer on single clear-cut solutions for the fashioning of production and work. Such tendencies are set up by scientifically produced uncertainties, and by the existence, in practically every field of action, of alternative models and expert opinions that compete with one another for a subpoliticization of economy and work. For

> the multiple possibilities that emerge amid a networking of structures and effects always entail a growth of uncertainties and ambivalences. Since allowance has to be made for more and more possibilities and

75

side-effects, it becomes more and more difficult to give a purely positive definition of certain goals and solutions and to present them as unavoidable constraints. This is true at the most diverse levels. In many innovatory projects, for example, there are disputes over whether they will cause more harm than good or raise more problems than they solve. The same holds for transport projects, or decisions to promote certain kinds of energy instead of others – and even if a certain objective is not disputed, there are usually various ways of achieving it, whose comparative advantages and disadvantages can only exceptionally be calculated in such a way that a clear vote emerges in favour of one option.[51]

On the other hand, the 'Fordist consensus' included the economic-political compromise of the 'worker-citizen'. This compromise, with its faith in rising living standards, left class-struggle rhetoric hanging in the cloakroom and sought to procure a commitment to democracy outside work in the electoral arena. But now, in the wake of the globalization and individualization of work, the Fordist worker-citizen sees the ground slipping away beneath his feet and becomes politicized. The key questions today are thus different. How will democracy be possible beyond the full-employment society? How should the right to discontinuity in employment be created and socially protected? How, and to what extent, can the development and basic funding of a civil society responsible for itself complement or even replace the state monopoly of public expenditure? This will be spelt out below in relation to work, and at least a start will be made in thinking through its biographical, social and political implications: first the Brazilianization of the West, then political society from a cosmopolitan point of view.

Multi-employment and the open organization of work

There is no doubt that the risk regime determines and identifies economic activity under conditions of world-open markets and competition. Depending on whether the dollar rate of exchange goes up or down, interest rates rise or fall, East Asian or South American banks and markets totter, whether Greenpeace intervenes and consumers stage an eco-revolt, whether governments raise petrol prices and lower speed limits, whether companies market new products, merge or split or suddenly vanish – according to all these factors, the order-book situation, investment decisions and management strategies change from one year to the next, from one quarter or sometimes even one week to the next. The risk regime means that, in principle, everything is possible and nothing can be foreseen or controlled. In this world of global risks, the Fordist regime of standardized mass production on the basis of a rigid, segmented and hierarchical division of labour becomes a key obstacle to the valorization of capital. When demand is both quantitatively and qualitatively unpredictable, when markets are globally diversified and therefore impossible to control, when information technologies make possible new modes of decentralized as well as globalized production, the conditions no longer exist for standardized production and work, as this was formulated in Taylor's 'scientific management' and taken over by Lenin for the Soviet philosophy and organization of work. For the rigidity of the Fordist regime drives costs up too high.

When demand increases, companies have to bring in expensive extra shifts. In slack periods, surplus products – cars, for example – have to be parked in their tens of thousands on company premises and can be sold only at reduced prices; or else output is cut by means of short-time working and lay-offs. Expensive social plans have to be constructed in lengthy negotiations. New products ultimately mean corporate arrangements – hence closures and new start-ups. All this can be avoided or minimized, if the risk regime of open world markets is successfully translated into the regulation risks of open work organization and employment conditions. In this way, the legal and biographical form of work changes from standardized security to deregulated risk.

The employment system that took shape in Europe over the past hundred years, partly through fierce social conflicts, rested upon a high degree of both temporal and spatial standardization of work contracts and labour deployment. With risk regulation, what is now developing is a destandardized, fragmented, plural 'underemployment system' characterized by highly flexible, time-intensive and spatially decentralized forms of deregulated paid labour.

As a result, the boundaries between work and non-work are starting to blur, in respect of time, space and contractual content; paid work and unemployment are spread over larger spaces and therefore become less and less socially visible from positions on the margins. Instead of company-structured labour densely packed into sky-scrapers and factories, a type of spatially diffuse corporate organization is appearing which, both outwardly and inwardly, can no longer be clearly defined in respect of markets, products, customers, workers and entrepreneurs. The same is true of unemployment. It too is becoming invisible, as it 'seeps away' into the no man's land between employment and non-employment. In the end, none of this is fundamentally new. The invisibility of the coordination of capital is 'simply' transferred to the level of work organization – with similar gains for management in new organizational and networking possibilities.

Flexibilization of working time: less money, but more control

The harmonization of the economic risk regime with the risk regulation of employment is strikingly illustrated by the labour-time models that match company order-book situations with employee time-budgets. As a rule of thumb, we may say that there are now almost as many labour-time models as there are companies. No one of them is like any other: all follow the pattern of the lungs, breathing in and out according to the order situation and the demand for employment.

> The Ford plant in Cologne, for instance, breathes with the help of so-called time-accounts. Employees work 37.5 hours – although the collective contract in the metalworking industry specifies 35 hours – and in return are credited with 2.5 hours a week in their time account. Furthermore, they can be called in for another 70 hours a year of assembly-line or office work, which are also entered in their account. When there is less work to be done, the workers withdraw time from their account as if it were money – and obtain free days off. 'In this way, we can respond optimally to fluctuations in the amount of work', explains Richard Goebbels, personnel manager at Ford's Cologne. . . .
> Nowadays, when the number of orders rises or falls at Opel Rüsselsheim, working time is adjusted without a hitch. 'Time corridor' is how Opel calls its model. The working week has almost no

core hours. It can last anywhere between 31 and 38.75 hours. The order situation is what decides. Things are similar at Audi, where the instrument is regular Saturday work. If orders go up in spring, for example, four extra Saturdays are worked and Audi does not have to pay any extra. In return, four Fridays off are awarded in autumn, when demand is known from experience to be lower. . . .

At IBM the most recent acquisition is called 'working time on trust'. Here there are no longer time accounts or corridors. Everyone checks their own working hours. Each worker is allocated a total number of hours for a particular period – but it is up to them how they distribute their individual time by day or by night, at home or at the company. . . . What is new about this flexitime is that employers no longer have to pay for output adjustments. On the contrary, employees receive no extra pay for temporary increases in work.[52]

Many suspect that major effects on social life and coexistence are bound up with the flexibilization of working time; that individuals will now roam around without fixed ties. Yet the historic experiment that Volkswagen tried at Wolfsburg with its four-day-a-week flexitime does not confirm these fears. Of course, the wonderful 'machine' that made Wolfsburg a community of like-minded people enjoying much the same level of provision is coming apart in the rhythm of flexible working hours. But the idea that 'flexible people' are now whizzing around town on Inline skates, that marriage and life together are being destroyed by the four-day week, has not stood up to the first painstaking sociological studies.

> The four-day week, says the marriage counsellor, has spent some time on my couch. People had more time and initially more problems. Mounting conflicts broke out in traditional marriages when the husband suddenly wanted to have a say in the children's upbringing and household arrangements, and the wife defended her domain. It eventually came down to a power struggle. Shorter working time requires adjustment, says the marriage counsellor. But I cannot see that more divorces are the result. On the contrary: those who have got used to it find that they have more time for family and hobbies.

Sceptics assume that there have been setbacks in the leisure sector. But the Volkswagen experiment suggests the opposite: double-digit annual growth-rates. This is what the local travel agent reports:

He books Majorca for well-off early pensioners, faraway destinations for flexitime workers, sometimes for as long as six weeks. They now have more free time and can take it as a block. Where else do you get that? The travel agent leans across the table and whispers: Bangkok is the same as ever. I'm not going to sit in judgement – it's what people pay us for.

But do people on flexitime perhaps lose interest in reading?

Naturally we thought things might soon look like they do in the Ruhr, says the owner of Wolfsburg's largest bookshop, Jens Großkopf. But that didn't happen. As a bookseller, he learnt from the trade what was going on in society. The four-day week strengthens categories five and ten. Five is travel, ten is health, do-it-yourself and hobbies. It used to be Fontane and Böll, says Großkopf, now it's asthma and Tenerife.[53]

Cutting costs not heads: flexibilization as a policy of redistribution

Of course, neither the spatio-temporal nor the contractual destandardization of paid work applies uniformly or simultaneously to all branches of the employment system. Even today there is no telling where this destandardization will run up against material and/or political limits, and which functional areas (and thus occupations, sectors, departments) will remain untouched by it. But it can already be said that flexibilization will not be income-neutral. As working time is divided up (not to support overemployment but to generalize underemployment and to mop up unemployment), there is a downward redistribution of income (as well as social security and career opportunities), in the sense of a collective decline across specialisms, occupations and hierarchies. Working-time policies are thus in a way always redistributory policies, and they create new insecurities and inequalities in society. This is undoubtedly the main reason why they encounter trade-union resistance and the active support and encouragement of many employers. This holds true even when flexible forms of underemployment arouse great interest among (especially younger) men and women, because they make it possible to achieve greater time-autonomy and a new and better coordination of paid labour and domestic labour, of work and life.

Once more, the experiment at Volkswagen-Wolfsburg may serve to illustrate this policy of redistribution. In the early 1990s, as crisis symptoms became sharper, costs exploded and fewer and fewer people wanted a Volkswagen, it suddenly happened that there were 15,000 too many workers on the payroll. Yet the company's top executives decided that they would not break with the principle of never declaring redundancies. Instead, plans were hatched to make labour cheaper through more profitable redistribution: 'Costs not heads', was the slogan. This meant full utilization of the company's capacity, with employees working 20 per cent less for 15 per cent less pay. There were a lot of disputes, fears and worries: either over living standards, or over the future influence of the unions and works councils. But in the end these fears proved to be no more than a passing episode. 'The wage reduction was somehow all right,' says one worker today. 'We complain about losses, but at a high level.' Since the wage cuts, people still earn as much at Volkswagen as elsewhere, but in four instead of five days. So this real-life experiment is not a transferable one.

According to the most comprehensive survey of its kind ever conducted, the Volkswagen workforce has largely accepted the new world of work.[54] Only 16 per cent of respondents stated that they were 'dissatisfied' or 'very dissatisfied'. Surprisingly, it was workers in the lowest income bracket who were most taken with the new model of work. Dissatisfaction grows with income: the less skilled value job security, whereas the highly skilled complain that they have to work more in less time – 'output intensification', it was called. The assumption that loss of income would be the main problem with a 28.8-hour week was not confirmed. Rather, the more attractive the work model, the more prepared people were to accept a major reduction in working time. Women, especially if they have children, are plainly more satisfied than men, and younger employees accept the new model more readily than older ones do.

With the deconcentration of space, however, the greater control that workers achieve over their work may go together with a privatization of the associated risks to health and psychological well-being. Safety norms tend to elude public control, and the costs of breaching or respecting them are shifted on to the shoulders of the workforce (just as companies save on the central organization of work – from building costs to the upkeep of machinery).

Low-cost academic jobs

Fragmentation of the time and place of work is compounded by fragmentation of the normal labour contract. This contractual individualization, with the introduction of cheap-rate insecure jobs, is taking place not only at the bottom but right at the top of the skills hierarchy, as the following example shows.

There no longer seemed to be anything standing in the way of Keith Hoeller's academic career. By 1982, when he netted his doctorate in philosophy, he had already contributed to ten academic publications, obtained a grant from the French government, and worked for a year as a visiting professor at the University of Seattle. He was even on the advisory board of a renowned specialist journal – an honour usually accorded only to full professors. And yet the decisive breakthrough failed to come. Over the past sixteen years he has stumbled from one fixed-term appointment to the next. His latest stop is a college in Washington State, where he gives twelve lecture courses a year – on a part-time basis. The job only brings in $26,000 a year. Now aged fifty, he suspects that his dream of a Chair will never be fulfilled. He has not even been given an office to himself. For part-timers are welcome cheap labour in America's universities, which suffer from diminishing budgets and sharper competition. Roughly 45 per cent of university teachers share Hoeller's fate, twice as many as in the 1950s.

The colleges save in several ways at once: the pay is only 40 per cent or so of a regular professor's; the sizeable pension and health contributions do not apply; and part-timers, unlike professors with tenure, can be hired and fired. This makes it possible for colleges to react swiftly and flexibly to changing preferences on the part of their customers, the students.

It is a good deal for the universities, but it splits the country's faculties into two classes. Keith Hoeller feels 'underpaid and overworked'. Only his presence in the lecture room is remunerated. He does not get a cent for the hours spent marking exams and preparing courses. He even pays his own petrol costs – as do many part-time lecturers who commute every day between three or four universities.[55]

In Germany, for the private sector at least, similar possibilities have been opened up by the Employment Promotion Act. Initially conceived as a temporary measure, this provides the legal basis for deregulation of the labour market (fixed-term contracts, job-sharing, labour available on call, casual labour), and hence for the individualization of paid work.

The downsizing of both skilled and unskilled labour also takes place on the basis of the '50/50' rule in the contemporary US economy, according to which people over 50 years of age and earning less than $50,000 a year are the first to be hit when jobs are divided or eliminated.

McJobs

What does it actually mean when someone earns so little that two or more jobs are needed to make a living?

Ursula Münch has a long day ahead of her: two jobs (one for eight hours, one for two); four bus journeys, involving twelve transfers and a total of three hours' travel; plus shopping, cleaning and cooking for the children. She is always in a hurry, and usually ends up running to the bus stop. Being in tax band V, she takes home 800 deutschmarks from her full-time job at McDonald's in Wiesbaden. She earns 610 marks from a side-job cleaning in a Wiesbaden council office. Her husband makes 2200 marks after deductions as an industrial salesman, so they are able to make ends meet.

Ursula Münch is strikingly serious. She does not laugh much. 'Things are all right for us', she says in every conversation. But what you keep stressing like that obviously does not go without saying. If Mr and Mrs Münch only put in normal working hours, they would fall below the income support level and be entitled to a monthly supplement – according to Wiesbaden Social Security. But the Münchs have never applied for that. She would rather do extra cleaning, even if it means dozing off on her feet during a bus journey. On weekdays Mrs Münch only sees her husband at night, asleep. When she gets up in the morning, he is already gone. And when he comes home, she is already behind the counter at McDonald's. She allows herself the extended workday of a top manager, simply so that she can say: 'We've got everything we need.' That includes rent, car and clothes.

This is a world of work about which many people are completely ignorant. In high-wage Germany there are some sectors where even full-time employees fall below the income support threshold – especially if there are children to feed. The success story of a company like McDonald's Deutschland, which has built 870 restaurants over a period of 27 years, was made possible only by low wage levels (currently DM10.72 an hour). Thomas Heyll, director of the German Catering Association – to which Pizza Hut, Burger King and McDonald's all belong – offers the following advice to employees with a net income below DM1500: 'Either work longer than the standard hours, or look for one or more extra jobs.' This also seems normal to Peter Dussmann, a Schwabian services provider who employs more than 37,000 people worldwide.[56]

All around the world, flexible work and insecure terms of employment are growing faster than any other form of work. In Germany between 1980 and 1995, the proportion of dependent employees in regular work situations fell from 80 per cent to approximately 68 per cent. In the early 1970s, there were still five regular employees for each one outside the standard terms and conditions. By the beginning of the 1980s the ratio was 4:1, by the mid-1980s 3:1, and by the mid-1990s 2:1. If this trend continues, the ratio in fifteen years' time will be 1:1. Only a half of employees would then have a long-term job protected by labour and social legislation.

The German Institute for Labour Market and Occupational Research estimated that in 1995 there were 1.5 million people self-employed in name only. In a third of cases, this involved activity additional to a regular job.[57] More and more often, editorial assistants, messengers, insurance brokers and lorry drivers have their employment terminated and then go on working at their own risk, but still in a relation of dependence upon their 'old' employer.

Estimates of the scale of this 'grey' work climb ever higher. The economist Friedrich Schneider suggested a figure of DM560 billion for 1990.[58] Opinions differ about how this is distributed among those with a main job and those who are otherwise unemployed. But it is often supposed that most of the grey work comes from the army of the unemployed. One survey found that 63,000 out of a sample of 70,000 unemployed did some work on the side.[59] This trend, which the Bavarian-Saxon Commission for Issues of the Future has documented in the case of Germany, appears to be broadly typical of the early industrialized countries. It is true that for the United States there are no exact and consistent series of figures for the number of people in a non-standard work situation. According to OECD statistics, however, nearly a quarter of employees in the United States in the mid-1990s worked part-time or had no job security or both – compared with a fifth in 1982.[60] Interestingly enough, it is precisely in the high-tech sector that many companies have recourse to non-standard forms of labour, especially 'permanent temporaries'. In 1986 there were 800,000 of these in the United States, but the figure had grown to 2.5 million by 1992. That is approximately 2 per cent of the economically active population. Estimates confirm that these 'permanent tempo-raries' now make up 10 per cent of the workforce in a fifth of companies – especially in leading high-tech firms such as Microsoft and AT&T.[61]

The possibility of dividing and recombining work in relation to specific tasks and goals, at any time or place, has created a sphere of power for virtual companies. For some time now, the reality and efficacy of this sphere have been growing even where the old institutional safeguards of the full-employment society still appear to be intact. But the threat of virtuality is everywhere present. As the boundless mobility of capital encounters institutional and cultural 'labour rigidities', which vary in form and legal character from country to country, the dominant trend is a real-life experiment to carry the flexibility of labour beyond all limits of time, place and contractual obligation. What distinguishes the risk regime, therefore, is not a division of society into winners and losers – for that has been true of all societies down the ages – but rather the fact that the rules of winning and losing become unclear and hard for individuals to grasp. Ultimately, the flexibility regime tells us: 'Rejoice that your knowledge is obsolete, and that no one can tell you what you will have to learn so that you are needed in the future!'

Risk regulation generalizes not only social insecurity but also cognitive and moral uncertainty about the rules. And new dilemmas appear on the scene. Never before has individual creativity been as important as it is today, when product innovation depends upon the creative application of new science and information technology. But never before have working people, irrespective of their talents and educational achievements, been as dependent and vulnerable as they are today, working in individualized situations without countervailing collective powers, and within flexible networks whose meaning and rules are impossible for most of them to fathom.

Eyes-closed politics and criminalization

The new diversity of temporary work is highly explosive in political terms. Any policy that seeks to restore the world of regular work has only three ways of going about it: eyes closed, criminalization and channelling. An eyes-closed policy (or non-policy) was taken to absurd lengths by the Kohl government in Germany, but it is well enough known that breaches in the dyke cannot be repaired in that way. Precisely when nothing is happening politically, a great deal happens out there in the world. Thus, within ten years the number of so-called marginal employees soared from 2.8 million to 5.6 million. The consequences are plain to see. Where mini-jobs without social obligations are no longer the exception but the rule, the old social security system is giving up the ghost. Eyes-closed policies condone and accept an insidious move away from the welfare state.

Anyone who 'deliberately' bets on full employment soon turns to a politics of criminalization, directed against 'swamping' by 'deviant' forms of employment. 'Just look at the mess everything is in,' complains the new minister for family affairs, Christine Bergmann. 'In Berlin there is any amount of grey economy work, wage-dumping and spurious self-employment. People say bye-bye to the social insurance system, even if they are in work. . . . Those are not hybrid forms; they are breaches of the law that might also be called exploitation.' The conclusion is that 'illegal' employment should be prohibited, spurious self-employment ended, the 'abuse' of DM620 jobs prevented, and social security contributions enforced even for the cheapest jobs. Indeed, the new Schröder government has built its programme on this. Labour Minister Walter Riester looks to a carrot-and-stick policy of channelling plus criminalization. 'It's not a question of going back to what used to be the normal work situation,' says Riester. 'But we cannot just idly look on when the old systems no longer function and their rules are even intentionally flouted. Diversity itself needs rules.' But which rules? Most answers to this question overlook the 'social rationality' that underlies the farewell to normal work situations. This should be seen as a 'circle of informalization': that is, as a self-reinforcing tendency and significance of informal work and economics under the conditions of the risk regime.

Justice deficits of the caring society

The big question is how labour can be cheapened so that more jobs are created, while at the same time the mutually supportive bonds of social security are renewed and the costs (or savings) are fairly distributed. What can be more obvious than to extend social insurance contributions? But this has paradoxical effects, since cheap-rate jobs would then lose what makes them so attractive to employers – low costs and easy availability. If such jobs are exempted from flat-rate (20 per cent) taxation and social insurance contributions are collected instead, this will certainly arouse the protests of the main recipients of tax revenue – the *Land* governments, in the case of Germany. At the same time, however, it is not clear where is the justice in non-taxation that favours a single mother with a job at McDonald's as much as it does an industrialist's wife who wants to earn something extra for herself. And if social insurance contributions are to be paid, why should not the contributors also be entitled to claim a state pension? Of course, the government avoids such a conclusion like the plague. It would wear down the caring society, because low personal contributions would ultimately entitle people to high benefits. But it must also be asked why many employees have to pay full contributions for cover they do not require at all, since they are insured in another way as pensioners or students.

The rule is the exception

The reality of work – and this is an understatement if ever there was one – is becoming more and more obscure. Yet the state requires clear categories to reach out and define people. How can these two facts be combined? By making the exception into the rule. This means hot air – a lot of bluster without any action, a perfect example of symbolic politics of which the best that can be said is that it is driven by ignorance and good intentions. The whole matter is obviously jinxed, because apparently identical kinds of work conceal opposite realities that no one is able to reduce to a common denominator. In catering, office cleaning and the retail trade, temporary work is by now largely the rule. To eliminate it is to endanger that whole area of the economy, and with it the jobs that one supposedly wants to create.

According to one of the plans devised by the labour ministry, holders of mini-jobs will pay more than DM300 into the health insurance fund – but only if they are already insured anyway (through the family, for example). If they are not so insured and earn between DM300 and DM620, the employer must pay his bit into the health fund – but no insurance cover results from it. The same applies to unemployment insurance. Seasonal labour is not affected by any of this, and exceptions are being discussed for a whole series of occupational groups such as newspaper-deliverers. Is that all clear? Attempts to cast rules for the rulelessness of non-standard labour soon turn into real-life satire.

Paradoxical coalitions/collisions

One can grumble with the best of arguments about the cheap new jobs, and even brand them as part of the exploitative strategy of global capital. But one should not be surprised if the very people one wants to protect turn around and scratch one's eyes out. Cheap-rate jobs are mainly women's jobs (more than 80 per cent in Germany). They are done by women in very different situations: by single mothers, for example, who have built their life around caring for their children; but also by married mothers who are sick of the sight of their four walls and simply want to get out and achieve some recognition for themselves, perhaps even putting a lot of their extra income into the care that then becomes necessary for their children. One way or the other, these are archetypal Social Democratic voters – ordinary people of the new precarious centre – who are now being criminalized as representing 'deviant' forms of work A regulation-mad politics soon runs into the paradoxical phenomenon that the protected attack their protectors, but also – as the other side of the coin – defend their 'exploiters'. Hence a 'perverse' coalition of 'exploiters' and 'exploited' may easily be convicted of solidarity in uncaring behaviour. For do they not join in tacitly breaking the rules of the caring society, and in abusing those who, whether employers or employees, moan and groan yet do fork out their social contributions?

For a long time now, any policy that intentionally eliminates low-cost jobs has not thereby removed the need in the economy or among the population for work of that kind. Criminalization is thus tantamount to a self-fulfilling prophecy. It hastens the movement into irregular work in the informal economy, which it then brands as criminal.

Cheaper services for groups with declining incomes

Formal services (because of high taxes and charges, among other things) are becoming prohibitively expensive for sections of the population with declining incomes who still want to maintain their standard of living. The informal economy is thus seen as a boon by these groups.

Informalization as a strategy of corporate rationalization

The spread of casual labour, spurious self-employment and 'permanently temporary' work offers many advantages for a strategy of corporate rationalization. It reduces wage costs, increases flexibility and shifts the burden of risk on to the workforce.

Relegation and intractable dilemmas

With the spread of non-standard forms of work and underemployment, there is greater pressure on individuals to offset their loss of income by working longer hours, mostly in spurious forms of self-employment or through part-time jobs on the side. Underemployment and informal work thus widen the demand for underemployment and informal work. For the same individuals taken collectively, however, this is a damaging form of behaviour. For it increases the supply of flexible temporary labour and weakens the individual's position in the grey economy, resulting in a further loss of income. 'If there are no mechanisms to limit cost-cutting competition among the suppliers of labour, a danger arises of self-reinforcing processes of impoverishment.'[62] And this arises as a result of work. Work and poverty, which used to be mutually exclusive, are now combined in the shape of the *working poor*.

Unemployment, non-work, grey work

Unemployed people have a lot of time on their hands and are financially very insecure. But paradoxically, their receipt of unemployment benefit obliges them to do nothing. They might almost be compared to thirsty people who have to promise not to drink one drop of extra water, because they are officially given one glass a day to moisten their parched throat. Otherwise they are 'social cheats', whose transgression is harmful to the public good.

This vicious circle – contradictory regulations, paradoxical coalitions, high-cost services, income loss, informality as a rationalization strategy, surplus time and deep financial insecurity of the unemployed – encourages the further spread of grey work and the informal economy.

Unless the informal economy is decriminalized, the problems of the labour market can hardly be successfully tackled. But then the dykes may possibly break. The Either-Or policy – either work and a wage or no work at all – means that the new risks of informality are heaped on to the shoulders of people in work. On the other hand, of course, the state cannot simply withdraw from the fray or even embrace the erosion of normal work and of the associated systems of social security. Consequently, politics is trapped between the criminalization and the recognition of informal work.

A structural pessimist might conclude that a policy of preventing the breakdown of normal work faces the intractable problem that all three options – closing one's eyes, criminalization and channelling – see the future lying with cut-price jobs. We shall see later that this does not at all have to be the case. For the moment, it should simply be noted that this conclusion holds only in relation to the norm of lifelong full-time work; and that there is also a life beyond high-pressure work and mass unemployment. To be successful, an alliance for labour 'would have to be expanded into an alliance for voluntary non-participation in paid work', as Martin Kempe has argued. This means that there would have to be a right to breaks in work, which would allow both women and men to work out their own way of switching between different fields of activity (paid work, family work, civic labour).

Summary

Those who kick up a fuss only about open unemployment fail to see the really new phenomenon that is drawing 'ultramodern' and 'premodern' countries closer together: namely, the replacement of standard with non-standard forms of work. Economic growth in today's world-market conditions is rendering obsolete the idea of classical full employment, lifetime jobs and everything that went with them. This is quite apparent in industrial production, but in usually more concealed forms it is also taking place in the knowledge sector of the service society, where many see hopes of new attractive jobs for all. It is precisely at this leading edge that automation, restructuring, dissection and relocation are the order of the day, amid ever new waves of rationalization to which there is no end in sight. Whatever politicians may promise, no amount of invocations of the good old full-employment society will change this tendency.

The publicly celebrated faith in a return of full employment is, however, extremely effective in its way. For it allows public opinion and the world of science to avoid tackling terribly difficult issues – the need, that is, not only for action but for a new foundation of social existence. To argue instead for an American-style jobs miracle, based on an eternal model of economic orthodoxy, comes down to saying: 'Just swallow the bitter neoliberal medicine, and everything will be fine.'

6

A Thousand Worlds of Insecure Work

Europe's Future Glimpsed in Brazil

The question, then, is what people do with their time; where they get their living and their self-image from. This will look different over the next hundred years from how it has over the past hundred. A hundred years ago there was no unemployment; it is an invention of the late nineteenth century. Previously people led complicated lives. Even industrial workers usually still had some links to the land or to other activities in life. A time is now coming in which we shall again move into different ways of living – not all of us, but a growing number. These ways of living will be more akin to those which women have known in the last few decades than to those which have been typical for men: that is, they will not involve careers, but rather combinations of part-time work, casual contracts, unpaid work and voluntary activity for the public good – a whole range of things. What is crucial is that politics should make this fundamental change easier and not more difficult. But this is where politicians are failing. Their discourse still runs on antiquated tracks, while in reality people have long been travelling on different paths. The unemployed do not just sit around or queue up at the labour exchange; they also look for what might be called a portfolio of activities. Some of these are paid, others not. It is a completely crazy world, when measured against the rigid standards of the old work society. But this is a transition, and as long as it lasts it will be painful to many people – especially to men, who cannot get used to the fact that the rigid idea of a lifetime career opportunity will no longer mean much in the future.[63]

But the downward elevator effect into the world of job insecurity does not affect everyone equally. As in the past, it is true internationally that insecure and temporary forms of employment are increasing faster among women than among men. Women make up by far the larger part of the working poor, and for them in particular the systemic change that is opening up a grey area between work and non-work takes place as a descent into poverty. Nor does the growing number of men confronted with insecure and fragmented working lives result in any positive easing of the gender conflict. Indeed, in so far as the reign of the short term also undermines relations of partnership, love, marriage, parenthood and family, men suffer as much as women – and public life too dies out.

How can what is happening be understood? In a striking reversal, countries of so-called 'premodernity', with their high proportion of informal, multi-activity work, may reflect back the future of the so-called 'late-modern' countries of the Western core. This change in who predicts whose future is what I mean by the 'Brazilianization of the West'; it indicates a world that can no longer be understood according to the schema of core and periphery. Such an emphatic image may arouse suspicions of a reverse Eurocentrism, whereby Western measures of value and ideas of development are deconstructed with the aid of a negative stereotype called Brazilianization. It also exposes itself to the well-nigh insoluble problems of cultural comparison. But if this means that we can discuss (and criticize) only by reference to an ideal-typical content, what are we to understand here by 'Brazilianization' as an ideal type?

By way of self-criticism, and self-irony, it may be said that the Brazilianization thesis does appear at first sight to renew, through negative inversion, the romantic image that Westerners tend to have of Brazil. Whereas Europeans set off in the nineteenth century looking for a South American 'paradise', 'the German papers nowadays carry an almost ritual annual report on how many people were killed during the Rio carnival. Usually the reporter forgets to mention, however, that a large number of these are "mundane" deaths in traffic accidents, the carnival period also being peak holiday time.'[64]

Table 2 Part-time workers by sector of employment, 1992.

	Agriculture		Industry		Services		Total	
	in '000s	*Women as %*	*in '000s*	*Women as %*	*in '000s*	*Women as %*	*in '000s*	*Women as %*
EUR 15	1196	6.2	2874	75.8	17,063	85.1	21,113	83.5
B	7	71.4	42	78.6	416	91.4	466	89.7
DK	27	40.7	79	64.6	484	79.6	592	75.8
D	217	76.5	962	87.9	4067	90.2	5245	89.3
GR	67	65.7	30	33.3	78	68.0	175	61.7
E	81	58.0	80	70.0	567	80.6	727	77.0
F	208	71.2	275	79.6	2305	85.5	2791	83.8
IRL	9	44.4	12	50.0	84	78.6	104	72.1
I	254	63.0	242	57.9	743	73.9	1239	68.5
L	–	–	–	–	10	90.0	11	90.9
NL	70	64.3	234	50.9	1755	76.9	2284	72.9
A	2	94.7	48	83.9	220	90.6	270	89.1
P	93	54.8	55	65.5	181	75.7	329	68.4
FIN	23	42.4	20	50.3	127	70.7	170	64.5
S	28	62.0	131	61.8	859	86.3	1022	82.1
GB	110	61.8	665	79.9	5168	86.4	5954	85.2

Source: Myrtha B. Casanova, 'Frauenarbeit in Europa', unpublished manuscript, Barcelona 1999.

> Brazil's development is broken in many different ways and full of contradictions: economic development does not coincide with social development; individual regions and federal states have their own histories and are themselves anything but homogeneous; Brazilian political discourse often has little to do with reality; wishful thinking, belief in miracles and a longing for salvation can here be unproblematically dressed up and 'marketed' in 'modern' social and economic terminology. There is no stabilization programme without its professorial justifications, no election without its new saviours.[65]

Nevertheless, the Brazilianization thesis is precisely meant to counter stereotyping and to clarify the 'disorder of progress'.

Farewell to the Western universalism of the work society

Does the development of the structure of work have common, or even the same, features in all societies? Or do these vary with the cultural context? Talk of Brazilianization sets aside any assumption that the establishment of the Western work society (with its degrees of formalization or legalization and its hierarchy of economic sectors) is a universal process. For industrialization does not stipulate any particular social or political accompaniment; neither the structure of income and employment, nor the mobility and regulation of labour, nor the organization of interests, has to be of a certain kind for the industrialization process to occur. Rather, these aspects will depend upon the specific cultural conditions and the actors involved.[66] As we have seen, this pluralization of modernity becomes more pronounced under the conditions of the risk regime.

Whereas the Brazilianization thesis initially appeared to turn Western universalism around into a universalism of the South, it may seem that the informalization of work is now being invoked as a universal tendency of development. But that is a serious misunderstanding. The cultural context and conditions of informal work in Europe and South America are completely different in such important dimensions as family ties and provision, the role of the state, and the historical experience of wage-labour.

Furthermore, quite different histories as well as contemporary causes and dynamics underlie the surprisingly similar precariousness of work in the so-called first and third worlds. What appears the same means in Europe the erosion of labour rights, living standards and social security. These basic questions of cultural comparison cannot really be addressed here, but the transition from a teaching society to a learning society (to use Wolf Lepenies's expression) completes the theorem of a Brazilianization that is beyond either universalism or relativism. The implied openness of the future in all parts of the world rests upon the assumption that there are many paths to modernity – as many as there are ways of not reaching it. Two kinds of phenomenon are especially interesting here: first, developmental differences and oppositions that can no longer be overcome through evolution, but have to be studied and recognized as expressions of 'divergent modernities' (Shalini Rhanderia); and second, tendencies which, despite contradictory cultural developments, display surprising similarities. This paradoxical alikeness of heterogeneous cultural developments and ideas of modernity is addressed in the thesis of a Brazilianization of the United States and Europe.

Will Europe perhaps, after a short historical period of relatively stable development, now have to bid farewell to its cherished notions of 'social order' and its black-and-white distinctions between the good life and the bad? If – argues Pries – we in Germany learn to see how exceptional was the normality of a half-century of collective advance,

> then it becomes easier to study the paths and visions of paid work in a South American country, not mainly out of 'folkloristic curiosity' but out of a sense that we can use this knowledge in order better to understand and develop our own paths and visions of work. As the emphasis is removed from the 'normal work trajectory' and the 'normal working life', it always makes sense to consider social contexts in which work and income, identity and provision, are woven together in a different way.[67]

In this connection, it must be asked how the anarchic poverty of South America, including the social brutality with which the weakest and poorest are left to fend for themselves, is related to the bureaucratically produced and labelled destinies of poverty and unemployment in 'the iron cage of welfare-state dependence'. Is the latter the end-goal in which the former will be 'surmounted'? Or are they not two manifestations of evil from which lessons should be drawn, so that backward progression and forward regression do not simply take it in turns with each other? Is the wish to escape the discipline of wage-labour and to become 'one's own boss' really only an illusion, only a premodern remnant that disappears as society reaches the age of modernization, much as adolescent rebellion dies out with adulthood? Or are dreams of resistance expressed here – everyday utopias which, in a West that has been losing its fictions of full employment, should now be everywhere talked up again in the name of autonomy and 'planted' in the wage-labour cultures through large-scale programmes of re-education?

The future of informality

Crucial to the Brazilianization thesis is the fact that, for all the cultural oppositions and incomparabilities, the future of informality now dawning in the West has a long tradition in South America and can be observed there in all its ambivalence.

The Brazilian face of the risk regime is apparent in the radical transformation of work which, since the 1980s but most intensively in the 1990s under the influence of globalization, has delocalized the various forms of production and opened up the labour market to the political economy of insecurity.

> Some of the positive trends that emerged in the Latin American labour market in the 30 years (1950–1980) preceding the current crisis were to a large extent reversed in the 1980s, which saw an increase in unemployment rates, a sharp decline in wages, an increase in the informal and more marginal types of jobs, and crises in traditional forms of labour unionization and collective bargaining.[68]

The uncoupling of economic growth and corporate profits from better working and living conditions for employees also has its parallels in Brazil. The relative stabilization and upward trend of the Brazilian economy in the 1990s did not lead to any improvements in the labour market. There was, it is true, a decline in the rate of unemployment between 1990 and 1994, but this did not continue and even gave way to a twofold downward evolution that will most probably mark the future of work in this part of the world.

First, the growth of informal and temporary job arrangements, 'inferior' at once in terms of productivity, working conditions, contractual terms, social security and legal protection. The numbers of small-scale self-employed and home-workers rose from 40 per cent of the economically active population in 1980 to approximately 57 per cent in 1995, while at the same time workers employed in the public sector fell from 15.7 per cent to 13 per cent and employees in the large private corporations from 44 per cent to 31 per cent. Out of a hundred jobs created between 1990 and 1994, eighty-one were in the informal sector and in small companies. In 1995, according to the International Labour Organization, the proportion actually rose again to 84 per cent. Not quite 35 per cent of the economically active population are protected by some kind of social insurance. This situation is reflected in the low capacity of the Latin American economies to create productive and attractive jobs.

Second, the deregulation of labour relations has intensified and led to types of flexibility that elude the bargaining power of trade unions and strategically weaken them. The number of people within 'deviant' forms of flexible employment has risen to 34 per cent in Argentina, 30 per cent in Bolivia, 20 per cent in Colombia and Mexico, and more than 50 per cent in Peru.

In order to interpret these figures, however, it is crucially important to modify the sharp European division between hierarchically structured sectors of work, and to grasp the special shades of meaning that informalization has in the Latin American world of work. The formal/informal and modern/traditional distinctions, or the sectoral breakdown into agriculture, industry and services, are barriers to an understanding of the intersectoral, inter-categorial diversity of work that is typical of Latin America.

'Being your own boss' in a global world of opaque dependence

It is estimated that in Brazil and Mexico roughly half the population form an excluded sub-class, whereas the middle layers –

who are courted by all politicians in the West – are hardly a significant political quantity at all. This is how the Mexican political theorist Jorge Castaneda puts it:

> There is, of course, a middle class in Mexico . . . but it constitutes a minority: somewhere between a quarter and a third of the population. The majority – poor, urban, brown and often excluded from the characteristics of modern life in the United States and other industrialized countries (public education, decent health care and housing, formal employment, social security, the right to vote, hold public office, and serve on a jury, and so on) – mingles with itself. It lives, works, sleeps, and worships separately from the small group of the very wealthy and the large but still restricted middle class. . . . The decades after the Mexican revolution – through the 1950s, perhaps – provided some upward mobility, some mingling, certainly the advent of a new business elite and an emerging middle class. By the 1980s, Mexico was once again a country of three nations: the *criollo* minority of elites and the upper-middle-class, living in style and affluence; the huge, poor *mestizo* majority; and the utterly destitute minority of what was in colonial times called the Republic of Indians – the indigenous peoples of Chiapas, Oaxaca, Michoacan, Guerrero, Puebla, Chihuaha and Sonora, all known today as *el México profundo*: deep Mexico.[69]

And Ludger Pries reports that in Puebla, Mexico's fourth largest city with a population of roughly 2 million,

> when you ride in a taxi and talk to the driver, you can hear life-stories that sound strange to Western ears. It is not at all untypical that the taxi-driver used to be formerly employed as a lorry driver or had been an illegal immigrant in the United States, or even earned his living on the assembly-line at Volkswagen de México. He will then give this or that reason why he 'voluntarily' gave up that work situation, bought himself a second-hand Volkswagen Beetle from his severance pay, and set out to work as a taxi-driver 'on his own account'. Why does a not badly paid employee at the finance ministry voluntarily leave after fifteen years and open a small electrical workshop? Neither the taxi-driver nor the former ministerial employee who now repairs electrical machinery will tell you that he regrets the move and would prefer to be on a company payroll again. One stock answer is: 'I don't want to be locked up in a company; I prefer to be my own boss.'[70]

'Being your own boss' – that is a widespread utopia, even among a majority of people who by Western standards are underprivileged, and it is one in which the structures and values of 'normal' paid work break down. Such points soon meet the objection that they involve a kind of postmodern romanticism, which prettifies informal employment conditions or is taken in by neoliberal propaganda. But Ludger Pries, to his own surprise, came to the conclusion that the relationship between formal work and the great 'informal urban sector' is completely open in the eyes of the economically active population, and that anyway there is no clear hierarchy or relation of dependence between the two. 'We also recorded a disproportionately high number of voluntary moves from dependent employment to independent activity and a relatively stable biographical pattern corresponding to them, so that it is hardly sufficient to interpret the informal urban sector as a holding pattern in preparation for the formal sector.'[71]

Perhaps this result is not so surprising, however, if one drops the premise of the normal work situation in the countries of the North. In Europe, too, the cultural internalization of dependent paid work was achieved only through a painful and conflict-ridden process stretching over hundreds of years, one in which the rule of law and a welfare state that took some of the burden off the family were as important as the experience of regulated work relations with complementary leisure. In such countries as Brazil or Mexico, only a small minority of the economically active population can similarly look back over several generations of paid work; indeed, stable, formalized wage-labour (as workers or as employees) is still only a minority experience. Since a public system of social insurance (health, pensions, unemployment insurance) does not exist for most people in Latin America, a major role is played by the extended family and by corporate-paternalist relations of care and dependence. Here it makes no sense to speak of a 'normal' work situation as standard in either the formal or the informal sector.

Beyond the certainties of the work society

In Latin America there are thousands of impermanent work situations. For a Western observer, the job of street trader or itinerant saleswoman appears especially strange, but in that part of the world it is largely unclear what are people's actual conditions of life and work, what are their real motives, hopes and hardships. For their common lot is defined negatively: they often have no building or market stall from which to offer their goods or services (nor, it should be added, can they assert any legal claim to one). They do not do their job only on the street or in some other fixed place that has to be defended against competitors. They also go from house to house, trying to build up a lucrative network of regular customers for their precious wares. Even if they cannot formally assert either ownership or use rights, they often symbolically, and in their context quite legitimately, defend their own 'sales pitch'.

> The demands and risks, as well as the income opportunities, vary enormously in this section of the active population. At one extreme one finds the young, dependent self-made man selling expensive electrical equipment from a fairly solid stall (a metal construction with a roof against sun and rain), whose stable contribution to an informal interest group of street *vendedores* gives him a degree of protection against outside checks and interference. At the other extreme, one finds the older woman with a young child offering vegetables for sale from a wooden crate at an unauthorized pitch, who has to reckon with checks by council officials at any moment. Not only is her income lower; the perishability of her goods adds to her many other risks.[72]

In Europe too, if one looks beyond the fiction of full employment, it is necessary to use quite new ways of discovering what people live on when they do not have the security of paid work. To counterpose from the start formal work and less valuable informal work, even if this only seems to be for the purposes of analysis, is to remain tied to the model of 'normal-formal economy and employment' and thus to see everything and everyone else as an 'excluded residue'.

'The informal economy is thus not an individual condition but a process of income-generation characterized by one central feature: it is unregulated by the institutions of society, in a legal and social environment in which similar activities are regulated.'[73]

Informal modes of work are thus always unorthodox types of income provision – often in the grey area between 'legal' and 'illegal', which is not least a matter of point of view or 'social construction' between people at specific moments. Transposing this to Europe, we might say that the much-attacked 'swindling of the welfare system' is precisely a source of stability. For it allows those who would otherwise have no income at all to get at least a little something and then a lot more for nothing. In a way, this is already the basic insurance that many have envisaged for the multi-active citizen, for whom paid work is only one among several sources of material existence.

> Many young people might not be able to live at all if they did not wangle housing or some other benefit that was not intended for them. It really is a mad world, because the whole welfare system is still based upon the old world of work that is out of many people's reach. And these many must try to manage somehow in a not yet restructured world, and this works in part only because they keep up the pretence. For it is within the framework of the old world of work that they make sure of their entitlements and secure a basic income for themselves.[74]

On the cynicism of statistics: more hopeless, less jobless

When we compare Latin America with Europe's fixation on a US-style 'jobs miracle', it becomes clear just how double-edged the alternative to 'unemployment' can be. For to be (no longer) unemployed can mean either to have a job or to stand no chance of having one. Those who return to a formal work situation and those who drop out of society are both no longer 'jobless'.

Corresponding to these opposites are two strategies for the overcoming of unemployment: either to create jobs with the whole bag of economic policy tricks, or to open the trapdoors of society and discourage or frighten people by dropping them into freedom. The trained gaze, which knows all about the static construction of unemployment (and its statistical overcoming), fails to appreciate that the creation of conditions in which more and more people are excluded from society is also indirectly a most effective strategy for the overcoming of unemployment. In other words, the unemployed in a European sense of the term still have the security of a possible job, or even a claim to formal paid work, whereas most of the non-unemployed in a Brazilian sense are light years away from that.

Only in this way can one understand how in Latin America, where large sections of the population are excluded from society as an underclass, open unemployment has been relatively low (between 3 and 5 per cent in the three decades from 1950 to 1980). But this means that 'jobs miracle' must be extended to include the 'overcoming' of unemployment through exclusion – an 'unemployment miracle'. The informal sector changes the understanding not only of work but also of unemployment. The statement that there is relatively little 'open unemployment' in Latin American countries is ambiguous in a quite fundamental sense. On the one hand, it points to the huge potential of the informal economy to integrate people willing to work and to offer them some chance of making a living. Truly these countries have a remarkable capacity to absorb people amid soaring population growth and flight from the land. On the other hand, the label 'not unemployed' can only be described as cynical in a region of the world where most of the excluded underclass does not show up in the 'unemployment' statistics.

With regard to the Western view of unemployment as a scandal, this cynicism may even be turned to political use. For decriminalization and recognition of the informal economy might appear to some – at least as far as the statistical construction of reality is concerned – as precisely the royal road out of unemployment.

If one compares employment trends, the dynamic of the informal economy leaps to the eyes. Agricultural employment declined as the non-agricultural sector underwent considerable expansion, but within the latter the informal sector increased nearly twice as fast (120 per cent) as the formal sector (50 per cent). Prognoses for Latin America estimate that by the year 2000 informal employment will account for 40 per cent of the total.

The ascription of unemployment and exclusion

But what does 'unemployed' really mean? Officially there is a 'struggle against unemployment' everywhere in Europe. In reality, however, as a group of campaigners in Berlin complain, it is a struggle against the unemployed: 'To this end, statistics are falsified, pseudo-jobs created and techniques of harassment introduced in the guise of checks. As such measures are always insufficient, it is claimed that the unemployed are responsible for their plight. They are turned into "job-seekers", in order to force reality into line with the propaganda. . . .'[75]

According to Michael Lind: 'The chief danger confronting the twenty-first century United States is not Balkanization but what might be called Brazilianization. By Brazilianization I mean not the separation of cultures by race, but the separation of races by class.'[76]

The colonial history of Latin America is mirrored in this association of ethnicity and class affiliation. Silvio Zavalla, the leading Mexican labour historian, notes:

> In this way slavery, feudal dependence, forced labour and debt bondage came from Europe to the New World. . . . Conditions in the Indian surroundings were not the same as those which prevailed in European history, where these forms of labour had arisen. The main functions of these in America were to supply European settlers or their offspring with manpower, to exploit the mineral, agricultural and industrial resources of the colonies, or to provide for the comforts of city life.[77]

Similarly, in modern Europe the consequences of the deregulated labour market accumulate along with ascriptive features in the traditionally disadvantaged groups of women and foreigners. There is a lot of evidence that the shift from normal to non-normal work situations follows the lines of gender and ethnic inequalities, and thus extends to the process of social exclusion in all its drama.

Time poverty, have-nots and the civil society revolution

The stability of the postwar order in the welfare states of Europe mainly rested upon the promise and the experience of collective upward mobility, upon the 'Fordist consensus' in which people accepted factory work and discipline in return for greater income,

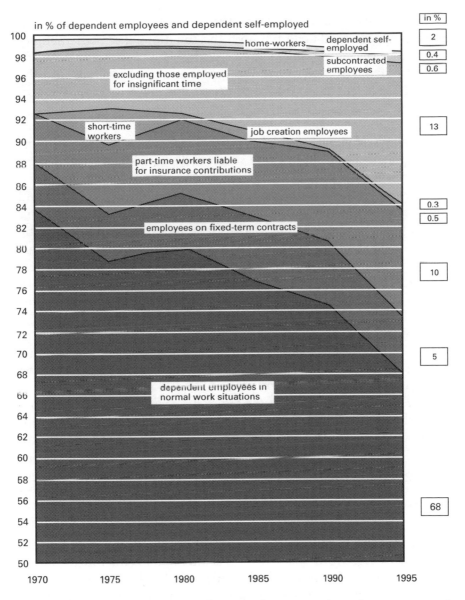

in % of dependent employees and dependent self-employed

Figure 1 Dependent employees in normal and non-normal work situations in Western Germany 1970–1995 (in diagrammatic form). © Campus Verlag.

social security and leisure time. This consolidation of a centre of society, which could underpin both the functioning of parliamentary democracy and a reform-oriented politics, is now being overturned by the Brazilianization of the West. If this trend continues into the future, there are likely to be four groups of people in Western societies.[78]

1   *The 'Columbus' class of the global age.* These are the winners from globalization, the owners of globally active capital and their top managerial executors. The income of this minority has been rising exponentially as a result of downsizing, wage compression and lower social contributions. Like Columbus, they set out to conquer global space and subject it to their economic goals. They are the money and knowledge elites, who have discovered the magic formula for the accumulation of ever greater wealth with ever less labour. They have the technological and material resources of globalization at their command – but they pay a high price for this in the form of time poverty. For the global elites lack what the most impoverished local rejects have in abundance: time. Moreover, as numerous studies have shown, there is a lot of coming and going among the rich. Those who are well off today will not necessarily be so tomorrow or the day after.

2   *Precarious employees at the top of the skills ladder.* These earn a lot, but have to be constantly on the ball to avoid being pushed aside by rivals. They are temporary workers, the spurious self-employed, people with their own business, and so on, in high-paid positions that assume similarly high educational qualifications. Things that used to be mutually exclusive – a good education and income and a tightrope-walking biography – here converge with each other. Underemployment and multi-employment are often two sides of the same coin: there can be no question of an eight-hour day. Leisure time is a foreign word, social life – 'vacations' – an endemic problem. Anyone who cannot be reached anytime and anywhere is running a risk. Such 'individual responsibility' lifts a burden from the public and corporate coffers and makes the individual the 'architect of his or her own fortune'.

3   *The working poor.* The jobs of 'low-skilled' and 'unskilled' workers are directly threatened by globalization. For they can be replaced either by automation or by the supply of labour from other

countries. In the end, this group can keep its head above water only by entering into several employment situations at once. They therefore experience what many others fear: freedom makes you poor! If the informal sector, in expanding, is not accompanied by public money for all, it can turn into a ghetto for the poor.

4 *Localized poverty.* Zygmunt Bauman has pointed out one essential difference from the poverty of earlier epochs: namely, the localized poor of the global age are no longer needed.[79] In the space-time diagram, their position may be thought of as complementary to that of the globalized rich. The localized poor have time in abundance, but they are chained to space.

In the United States, where this group of the socially excluded has grown considerably in the past twenty years, the concept of an 'underclass' has been explored in relation to it (Jencks, Katz, Wilson). Poverty is a major and necessary – but, most observers think, not sufficient – condition for someone to slip outside society. An underclass, they argue, is made up of those who have abandoned all hope of returning to society, and who therefore breach the fundamental rules of human coexistence. Many even speak of the 'anti-social' behaviour of this group of the isolated very poor, who have become the most important social challenge facing America. In the big inner cities, where the demand for unskilled labour has plummeted while the affluent and mobile middle layers have moved out, an underclass of chronically unemployed have-nots live off welfare hand-outs or criminal forays or both. So far, no social policy has come up with a solution for this growing group of people living outside society yet at the same time within it.

Such exclusion is often automatically equated with political apathy, but this is not an accurate picture of either Latin America or the United States. In both regions, there is lively debate about the 'civil society revolution' (Javier Gorostiaga): that is, about how the relationship between social self-organization, social movements, churches, trade unions, etc., on the one hand, and political parties, governments and states, on the other hand, looks now and could or should look in the future.

In Latin America today, leading figures in political life equate 'civil society' with 'social movement'. The Jesuit Javier Gorostiaga, for example, who originally comes from Panama, thinks that it is precisely civil society – consisting of peasants', workers' and women's organizations, environmental movements and grassroots Christian communities – which will form the building-blocks of the new democracy. As an example of the consolidation of democracy by civil society, he cites Haiti and the overwhelming electoral victory of Aristide's Lavala movement. Gorostiaga describes this movement as the 'concentrated power of the organizations and institutions of civil society'. Its further development was suddenly broken by the military seizure of power.[80]

The European understanding of civil society and direct democracy attaches a certain class or material status to the concept of 'citizen'. (This association is especially strong in the German language, where *Bürger* may mean either citizen or bourgeois.) Here, then, the concept of 'poverty' or 'exclusion' and the concept of 'civil society' are as opposed to each other as fire and water, and talk of civic democracy is very soon accused of expressing a middle-class bias.

The American political analyst Benjamin Barber, who heads a centre for research into the 'culture and politics of democracy', considers such attitudes to be quite misguided.

Here in America the middle class is pretty contented and does not get involved much; the poor have a greater tendency to commitment – not so much at elections as in local activities. Some time ago already, the civil rights movement organized without any support from foundations or other institutions. . . .

Of course, the socially underprivileged are capable of action. Even their abstention in elections is sometimes an active move: a sign of protest. And look at organizations like the Black Muslims. Whether you like it or not, their self-organization is a fact; they are capable of organizing, even in prison.

Research at the University of Chicago has shown that, in many ways, the educated middle layers simply do not perceive the organizational form of the poor. Colleagues from Chicago asked the residents of more than twenty housing blocks in the inner city ghetto, whether they belong to any community or association. And in those blocks, where hopelessness is supposed to be the rule, they have set up 320 organizations. But they are not like the ones we know so well; half of them were supported by Black Baptist communities, for example. You will hardly find them on the maps of city sociologists, which baldly state: 'Only gangs rule in the ghetto' – period.[81]

Thus, against the charge that talk of 'civil society' betrays a middle-class bias, Barber's riposte is that middle-class bias underlies the existing research on the social self-organization of the excluded.

7

The Great Example?

Work and Democracy in the USA

In this chapter, the thesis of a Brazilianization of the West will be discussed in the light of the US experience. Why is this taken as the example, and not another European country, or perhaps even Japan or the South-East Asian tiger economies? My answer is that, after the collapse of the bipolar world order that rested upon the opposition between communism and capitalism, the United States model was asserted as the model of 'Western modernization' with worldwide reach, indeed dominance. For many European countries, and especially for European corporations and business representatives, it is also the model of a flexible labour market – and one against which a European path, if there is one, has to differentiate itself. The US example also allows us to study, at their most advanced stage, the social and political consequences of the flexibilization of working time and location and the labour contract, and thus of the risk regime itself. For this very purpose, however, it is first necessary to consider the opposite tendencies that are also emerging on the horizon of cultural values and perception.

Freedom or equality?

All Western countries are similarly affected by the informalization and individualization of paid work. But this epochal change is per-

110

ceived and valued differently in different cultures. The creeping Brazilianization of the work society is variously seen and valued, praised or combated, according to the levels of toleration of social inequality, the prevailing notions of care and welfare, and the understanding of, and professed belief in, freedom and democracy. In the history of the twentieth century, the world economic crisis that broke out in 1929 made these differences strikingly conspicuous. In Germany, where the resulting mass unemployment was blamed on a 'systemic breakdown' of democracy, National Socialism became a mass movement virtually overnight, eventually enabling Hitler to capture power. Nowhere else was there a comparable reaction. In Britain and the United States, unemployment climbed as high or even higher, and the social effects were especially drastic in America, where welfare measures had to be improvised for the first time under the pressure of the jobs crisis. But the democratic institutions did not fall apart and came through undamaged.

American liberalism, Michael Walzer has argued, distinguishes itself by the most decisive emphasis on the rights of the individual, which means that the state is conceived as strictly neutral, without any cultural or religious project or indeed any collective goal beyond personal freedom and the physical protection, welfare and security of its citizens.[82] At the same time, Americans recognize and experience something like a 'national community' (much more chosen or elective than the German *Gemeinschaft*), which is what Gunnar Myrdal has called the 'American faith' and others, alluding to Rousseau, call a 'civil religion'. According to the ideal, this living faith in democracy and political freedom supersedes all the differences and oppositions of skin colour, religious denomination, income level, gender and political persuasion. It is true that there has been much talk of an Americanization of Germany since the Second World War, but it can hardly be said to have taken place at this cultural core level.

Take, for example, the results of the *Economist*'s comparative survey of value attitudes in Western democracies, which it presented under the revealingly Eurocentrist title 'An Odd Place: America'. When asked to say whether they valued 'freedom' or 'equality' more highly, Germans and Americans gave strikingly different answers. In the United States 72 per cent voted for freedom, and only 20 per cent for equality; whereas in Germany freedom was chosen by 37 per cent and equality by just under 40 per cent.

The interviewers probed deeper and asked whether government should intervene to bring about greater income equality. An overwhelming majority of Americans (80 per cent) said no, while very nearly 60 per cent of Germans said yes. As to Italians and Austrians, 80 per cent said they thought the state should balance out the injustice of poverty caused by the free market.[83]

In the perception and evaluation of freedom and equality, there is still today (for all the Americanization) a 'clash of cultures' between the United States and Europe. The central task of the state in Europe – the closing of inequalities due to the unfettered market – represents a principle exactly opposed to Isaiah Berlin's classical definition of the American concept of liberty: 'freedom from state interference' and 'freedom to do our own thing'.

The universal mission of the free market as America's belief in itself

With the collapse of the Berlin Wall in 1989 and of the Soviet empire shortly afterwards, the free-market utopia became the global mission of the United States, which no longer encounters any evenly matched opponent. 'Today's project of a single global market is America's universal mission co-opted by its neo-conservative ascendancy. Market utopianism has succeeded in appropriating the American faith that it is a unique country, the model for a universal civilization which all societies are fated to emulate.'[84]

This conviction that the world can revive itself through the free market has become the unofficial creed of America's civil religion. If the authority of American institutions really is global, and if the free market is part of the core of those institutions, then the free market must itself have universal application. In other words, not many capitalisms but the American way of capitalism sets the goals and standards by which other countries have to orientate themselves and be measured. All the more important is it to ask what effects and side-effects this far from modern, indeed rather archaic, ideology of the free market has unleashed in its civil-religious land of origin. How sustainable is the thesis of a 'jobs miracle' there? What are its darker sides?

Worrying signs in paradise

In the mid-1990s, per capita GDP in the United States – measured in 1991 purchasing power parity – was a fifth higher than in Germany; while the proportion of the population in gainful employment was a good 10 per cent higher, at about 48 per cent compared with 43 per cent. Hourly productivity, however, was a tenth lower in the United States than in Germany, and there was a strikingly low rate of productivity increase per person employed. Whereas GDP per head of the economically active population doubled between 1970 and 1994 in Japan and rose by two-thirds in West Germany, it increased by only a fifth or so in the United States. That was one of the lowest rates of increase in the whole of the OECD – and the other side of the coin of the country's high labour force participation.

The fact that so many of the new jobs are in sectors with low productivity – especially the retail and catering trade and small-scale services – casts a shadow over the American paradise. In the mid-1990s, 55 per cent of the US economically active population was employed in these sectors, compared with only 45 per cent in Germany. This difference already explains the entire employment gap between the two countries. If Germany were to catch up in retail services, it would have proportionately more employed and fewer unemployed than the United States.

The first shadow over the 'American way' is thus its well below average productivity in these sectors. More than half of those employed in this segment of the labour market are low-wage earners, compared with only a quarter in Germany. What this means, however, is that the tenth by which America's labour force participation exceeds that of Germany consists of low-paid jobs displaying low productivity.

Furthermore, incomes in this sector of employment are still evidently declining. Growing income inequality has led in the United States to millions of working poor; between 1973 and 1993, real hourly wages of those without a university diploma fell from $11.85 to $8.65. In the early 1970s, households in the top 5 per cent of the income pyramid earned ten times more than those in the bottom 5 per cent; today they get nearly fifty times as much. This sorry state

113

of affairs is now appearing in Europe too. Similar trends are evident in Britain and even in Sweden, the country with the strongest orientation to equality.[85]

The erosion of the middle class

America is not a land in which a well-off majority looks with concern at a desperately poor and excluded underclass. No: fear and economic insecurity also prevail among the majority. The United States is the only advanced country where productivity has constantly risen over the past twenty years, while the income of most of its citizens (eight out of ten) has stagnated or declined. The average weekly earnings of 8 per cent of Americans in gainful employment dropped by roughly 18 per cent between 1973 and 1995, from $315 to $258 a week. At the same time, the real income of top managers soared by 19 per cent in just ten years between 1979 and 1989.

Edward Luttwak remarks on this new insecurity of most of America:

> As entire industries rise and fall much faster than before, as firms expand, shrink, merge, separate, 'downsize' and restructure at an unprecedented pace, their employees at all but the highest levels must go to work one day without knowing whether they will have their job the next. This is true of virtually the entire employed middle-class, professionals included. Lacking the formal safeguards of European employment protection laws or prolonged post-employment benefits, lacking the functioning families on which most of the rest of humanity still relies to survive hard times, lacking the substantial liquid savings of their middle-class counterparts in all other developed countries, most working Americans must rely wholly on their jobs for economic security – and must therefore now live in conditions of chronic acute insecurity.[86]

Free-market utopianism, concludes John Gray, is not only a conservative project; 'it is the programme of an economic and cultural counter-revolution', pursued with the missionary zeal of America and meant to make the whole world happy.

114

Work and Democracy in the USA

The decay of social capital

Political dilapidation is advancing hand in hand with economic insecurity. The keywords of political discussion in recent years, especially in the United States, but also in Europe, Japan, South Korea, and so on, have been 'gloomy mood', 'tendency to protest', 'blocked reforms', 'policy breakdown', 'decline of political parties', 'erosion of communal ties and civic engagement'.[87]

In his classic work *On Democracy in America*, Alexis de Tocqueville already stressed that it cannot be an accident if the most democratic country in the world is precisely the one whose citizens have mastered the art of pursuing common goals that correspond to the common good. This insight, coming from the cradle of European modernity, gains new meaning everywhere today in the declaration of discontent that appears to have become characteristic of the developed Western democracies.

On the one hand, new studies impressively confirm Tocqueville's insight that both political institutions and economic activity can be successful only in so far as they can fall back upon norms and networks of civic engagement.[88] They live off this 'social capital', but in recent years they have also been reported as wearing it down – especially in the homeland of the 'jobs miracle'.

Electoral participation in the United States has fallen by nearly a quarter from its relatively high level in the early 1960s. At the elections to the Senate and House of Representatives in September 1998, it stood at no more than 38 per cent, itself up on the pollsters' predictions of a little over 30 per cent. The question therefore poses itself whether a democracy with a 30 per cent turnout at elections is still a democracy.

Over the past twenty years, the number of Americans who attend public meetings on community or school affairs has declined by more than a third. Similar falls have been visible in other kinds of political involvement: for example, written communication between citizens and members of Congress, or committee work for a local association. Each year 2 million people drop out of the formulation of public demands and objectives, or from church services and activities (down by roughly a fifth since 1960). Parallel reports come from the trade unions, whose membership figures have fallen by more than a half since the

115

1950s, from large voluntary organizations such as the Red Cross, and so on.[89]

These trends become explicable if it is borne in mind that political life decays with the spread of informal work. The 'jobs miracle' itself forces many Americans to take on more than one job to maintain their family's living standards, instead of the single one that used to be sufficient. As a result, millions are practically never at home any more: they live on the job and lack the time and energy that used to be available for voluntary commitments. In the 'circle of informal and insecure work' (see above), which compels those affected to work more for less, there is no time or air left for democracy.

The 'prisons miracle', or ethnicity as class

Ah, America! Who praises thy jobs miracle should not pass thy prisons miracle over in silence! As the US economic sociologists Bruce Western and Catherine Beckett have shown in a detailed study, the number of prison inmates tripled between 1980 and 1996. Some 1.6 million people, mostly young and overwhelmingly black, are sitting in cells and therefore outside the jobs market. At the end of 1994, the US incarceration rate was four times higher than Canada's, five times higher than Britain's, and fourteen times higher than Japan's. Only post-Communist Russia had more of its citizens behind bars. In Germany there are 80 prisoners per 100,000 adults, whereas in the United States there are more than 500. The risk of landing in jail is seven times higher for a black than for a white.

> The differences between countries are even greater if one narrows the focus to Afro-Americans. Their incarceration rate is more than twenty times higher than in Europe, and these values correspond to high absolute figures. . . . The objection might be raised that the penal structure in the United States has been more an inevitable reaction to high or rising crime than an active policy of intervention, although according to national statistics on victims, crime rates have been constantly falling since 1980. On the other hand, in contrast to

the crime figures, which are based on FBI reports and show rising crime-rates for some parts of this period, a thematic analysis of these and other data shows that the incidence of crime remained constant. . . . In any event, a recently published comparative analysis of data from a number of different sources comes to the conclusion that the United States is not the industrial democracy most affected by crime. Admittedly the murder rate in the United States is very high compared with other countries, yet convictions for homicide offences account for less than five per cent of the total number of jail sentences, so that the high murder rate in the United States does not explain the high rate of incarceration. Rather, it appears to be the result of more aggressive criminal prosecution, tougher sentencing, and broader criminalization of drug offences.[90]

This unparalleled rate of incarceration puts the jobs miracle in rather a different light. For it represents huge public costs that go systematically unreported, and tells us a sorry story about the situation within American society. Despite the claims that Europe is seizing up while the US labour market is successfully deregulated, the authors have calculated that the unemployment rate for US males between 1975 and 1994 was above the European average. And Jeremy Rifkin bitterly concludes: 'We also have a social net, only it is four times more expensive than the German one. It is called prison.' US unemployment figures are therefore subject to a 2 per cent upward revision. In the long term, the authors argue, the rate of incarceration will raise unemployment still further by worsening the job prospects for former inmates.

The wide discrepancy between black and white incarceration rates is an especially clear sign of how far Brazilianization has gone in the United States. Ethnicity and membership of the underclass reinforce each other. It is no longer so much that society is divided by various ethnic and religious identities, as that the ethnic feature of skin colour decides whether one is included or excluded from society.

John Gray argues that Samuel Huntington's thesis of a 'clash of civilizations' is precisely what psychology knows as projection: a danger looming within America's big cities and ghettoes, the danger of civil war among different subcultures, is projected on to the world as a whole. Gray, who teaches social theory at the London School of Economics and was formerly one of the leading Thatcherite intellectuals, takes this one step further:

117

It is no longer realistic to think of the US as an unequivocally 'western' society. There is much that points to its becoming, in a generation or so, one of the world's emerging post-western countries. Demographic trends suggest that in a generation or so there will be a near-majority of Asian, Black and Hispanic Americans. By the year 2050, according to the US Census Office, Hispanic Americans will outnumber the combined total of Blacks, Asian Americans and American Indians, and non-Hispanic Whites will have declined from 73.1 per cent of the population in 1996 to 52.8 per cent. As a consequence of these demographic changes, the United States will differ sharply from other countries in the Americas, such as Chile and Argentina, that remain unambiguously European in their ethnic mix and cultural traditions. . . . The old, East Coast elites whose worldview was shaped by the Second World War and the Cold War and whose cultural allegiances were Atlanticist have become already politically marginal.[91]

A critique of Chicago orthodoxy: neoliberalism serving the break-up of society

Those who claim to have a patent cure for the world's problems – namely, the detachment of the market from its cultural embeddedness and from political or legal regulation – are not speaking the truth. For a programme that ostensibly creates a work-paradise on earth is actually – often without this being intended or even noticed – a programme for the break-up of society.

The 'Fordist deal', which promised increasing prosperity for all, has been turned around into a policy for the break-up of the middle layers. The centre of society is being crushed to bits. The 'social capital' which alone makes economic and democratic action possible is falling apart. The political economy of insecurity prevails at the heart of society, even where hierarchies still persist in terms of education and income. The high-wire balancing act is becoming the paradigm for individual biography and social normality. Become a life-artist or go under: such is the alternative that is posed everywhere, and the two are not even mutually exclusive. Postwar social security is giving way to a risk society, a society of 'risky freedom', which redefines the equality principle as equal decline for all. Karl Marx's politically directed prognosis of social division is being fulfilled in a new way: the wealthy minority grows ever richer and smaller, while the great non-class of the excluded is becoming ever larger.

The neoliberal paradigm of politics may be said to involve an immanent contradiction: the power of the state and its institutions is supposed to be meticulously captured and applied to the breaking of that power. This is in a world where the collapse of national institutions in the 1990s has led to truly devastating human tragedies and civil wars in Somalia, East Africa, Yugoslavia, Albania and parts of the former Soviet Union, and now to the threat of turmoil resulting from the South-East Asian financial crisis. Even if the weakening of central state power cannot be solely or primarily attributed to the new influence of global markets, it nevertheless appears that under their pressure a hidden vacuum of state power and legitimacy may suddenly and brutally become apparent.

At a more detailed level too, one can study how the neoliberal revolution undermines its own foundations. Wherever it has been 'successful' – in the United States and the United Kingdom, for example – its effects have caused the political coalitions at its head to break apart and to hand over power to the opposition.[92] Evidently the neoliberals have not yet realized that the world has become democratic, and that electorates are not prepared to vote in politicians who have inscribed social decline or decomposition on their party banners.

Free-market utopianism is a kind of Marxism without Marx. Following the collapse of Communism, it seeks to realize Marx's prognosis of the division and destruction of society, but without any hope of emancipation through socialism. It thus negatively favours a neo-Marxism of hopelessness – for the same reason, namely that social collapse is threatened without any political alternative. At the same time, Europe is beginning to awaken from the shock in which it landed as a result of perhaps the only moment of joy in its long and joyless history, the peaceful collapse of Communist tyranny. The question of what constitutes politics is being rediscovered. What will be the goals of a European political union, once a common currency area has been created through the euro-experiment? What can fill the political vacuum left by the disappearance of the 'working citizen' who formed the core of the postwar consensus? How can the social safety-net continue after the end of the full-employment society? How can one prevent more and more people within society being excluded from society?

How can the global ecological crises be made the spur for new transnational forms of politics and democracy? 'Living one's own life' is the guiding image of our times. So how can the desire for self-fulfilment and self-determination be harmonized with the need of democratic institutions for participation and consent? In other words, the legacy of the bipolar world order raises the question of the recovery of politics. The less our vision is obstructed by the old conceptual ruins, the clearer it will become that the alternative facing the world is either collapse or political self-renewal.

8

Vision of the Future I
The Europe of Civil Labour

The great opportunity that arose with the collapse of the bipolar world order in 1989 lies in the fact that no one can lock themselves away any more from other cultures, religions and ideas; that all now share a space in which the old territorial identities and cultures, as well as the old frontiers and identities controlled by national states, suddenly encounter one another without protection. This helps us understand the globalization shock that has continued to affect the countries of Central Europe, and especially Germany since the fall of the Berlin Wall. The other side of our living in a more open world is the fact that there is no longer a *single* model of capitalism or a *single* model of modernity. There are many capitalisms, many modernities, which do, however, need to be brought into relationship with one another.

Multiple modernities and the mirror of one's own future

The self-transformation of the Western model, and of its claim to a monopoly on modernity, has made people in the West more open to the history and present situation of divergent modernities in all regions of the world. The framework that used to divide world society between highly developed and developing countries, a first and a third world, tradition and modernity, has been breaking apart. In the global age, non-Western societies have the same spatial and temporal horizon in common with the West. Indeed, their position as 'provinces' of world society is derived from the same challenges of the second modernity that are variously perceived, evaluated and addressed in different cultural contexts and locations.

In the first modernity, non-Western societies were defined by their strangeness and otherness, their 'traditional', 'extra-modern' or 'premodern' character. In the second modernity, where all have to position themselves in an identical global space and to confront the same challenges, the sense of strangeness is replaced by astonishment at the degree of similarity. This involves a self-critical move on the part of the Western project of modernity, which can no longer claim to be the pinnacle of progress or to have a monopoly on modernity. The extra-European world comes to be defined on the basis of its own history and self-understanding, and no longer regarded as the opposite or the absence of modernity. (Even today, however, many European social scientists think that a study of Western premodern societies is enough to make meaningful statements about the situation and problems of non-Western societies!) In the second modernity, many different cultures and regions of the world find themselves on different paths to different conceptions of modernity, which they can also fail to reach in different ways. The transition to the second modernity therefore sharply raises the problem of cultural comparison within different regional ('national') frameworks, and compels dialogue to begin among multiple modernities on the basis of their mutual recognition.

It is wrong, for example, to exclude non-Western countries from the framework of analysis of Western societies, with regard to the history and the contemporary reality of Europe. Shalini Randeria turns around the evolutionary hierarchy of Western and non-Western countries, arguing that – to stand Marx's judgement right side up – the 'third world' in many ways reflects back to Europe the image of its own future.[93] More specifically, this means that the West should listen to what non-Western countries have to say in relation to the following historical experiences.

▨ How can people successfully live beside one another in multi-religious, multiethnic and multicultural societies?

122

- Western societies can protect themselves against disappointment by means of realistic, non-utopian answers to the question: How is tolerant coexistence possible in a limited space, where cultural differences are present and liable to turn violent?
- Non-Western countries are also 'highly developed' in matters concerning legal pluralism.
- A previous lack may turn out to be an advantage. Thus, non-Western countries have experience of handling multiple sovereignties on a day-to-day basis – something that will also be typical of multinational Europe with its single currency area.

On the other hand, Western societies are starting to adapt to non-Western realities and standards from which scant good is to be expected:

- Deregulation and flexibilization of paid work are making normal in the West what for a long time counted as an evil to be overcome: that is, an informal economy or informal sector.
- Moreover, deregulation of the labour market tends to see off the corporately organized employee society, which used to pacify the class struggle between labour and capital by harmonizing a capitalist supply-side dynamic with a series of rights for 'working citizens'. With the informalization of labour relations and contractual conditions, union-free zones are also spreading to the heart of the Western post-work society.
- Many countries of the non-Western world are considered weak states. If the neoliberal revolution continues, legitimation crises with open violence akin to civil war may be studied as one aspect of the West's future that is already present in the countries of the South.

All this underlines two points: first, the urgency of a framework to analyse the world we inhabit under the risk regime, the world risk society, and to reveal the hidden connections, likenesses, oppositions and new lines of conflict between Western and non-Western countries; second, the need to break the spell of the work society

123

and to outline the basic features and visions of a European model for the post-work society.

What, then, is being opposed to the work society? Not a leisure society, but the vision of a society that is political in a new sense of the term.

Prelude to seemingly reckless optimism

I should like to convey here two messages, which at first sight have absolutely nothing at all in common. The first source is André Gorz: 'Any politics, whatever ideology it may invoke, is false if it does not recognize that there can no longer be full employment for all and that wage-labour cannot remain the main focus, or even the main activity, in everyone's life.' The other is Immanuel Kant: 'To think of oneself as a compatible member of world civil society in accordance with the laws of citizenship is the most sublime idea that man can have of his destiny; it cannot be thought without great enthusiasm' ('Reflexion 8077', *Handschriftlicher Nachlaß*). Despite their apparent distance from each other, these two messages have a common link that I should now like to uncover. The farewell to the work society will perhaps cause less pain and anguish if there is the prospect of successfully moving towards a (especially European) world civil society that is at once global and local. Elimination of the work society plus construction of Europe – that is a connection which can be made.

No one will leap into a void. To step away from the work society in the classical sense requires an attainable and enticing goal to be present on the horizon, capable of overcoming the pragmatic scepticism of a much-abused modern consciousness allergic to false promises. It is not a question of implanting something in that consciousness, or of somehow talking it round, but rather of awakening a still dormant hope, so that the sense of impossibility which has deadened it for several generations is completely overcome and a new gaze can be directed without shame at the hidden charms of the new.

A Europe of unemployment is simply a nightmare for many commentators. Many others deplore the abstractness of a politics which, in its national fixations, has lost sight of what is making people depressed and anxious: namely, such locally burning global issues as environmental destruction, refugee flows, poverty, homelessness, and lack of communication between cultures and religions. Hardly anyone notices that these two complaints or charges lose their basis if political society with a cosmopolitan intent, in a new everyday sense, takes the place of work-centred society – as a guiding idea.

The counter-model to the work society is based not upon leisure but upon political freedom; it is a multi-activity society in which housework, family work, club work and voluntary work are prized alongside paid work and returned to the centre of public and academic attention. For in the end, these other forms remained trapped inside a value imperialism of work which must be shaken off. Those who wish to escape the spell of the work society must enter political society (in a new historical meaning of the term) – a society that gives material form to the idea of civil rights and transnational civil society, and thereby democratizes and gives new life to democracy. This is the horizon and the programmatic essence of the idea of civil labour, which we now need to explain in more detail.

One major misunderstanding must first be cleared up. The point is not to recommend civil labour as a world-saving lifebelt, but to adopt the wise Chinese saying that the longest journey begins with a first step. Civil labour means the politics of the first step.

We Europeans are intellectual giants at picturing over and over again the endless chain of disasters and the impossibility of overcoming them. But we are dwarfs when it comes to laying solutions on the table, or even spurring people on to conceive and test a way out of the horrors. If there is a core to the postmodern consciousness, it is this sense of well-being in crisis, this feeling that the enemy is not the crisis but any notion that it might be overcome. Yet the passion for crisis rests upon a blind, unrecognized optimism, which in the end does not know or does not want to admit the real threat. The seemingly light-footed and light-minded optimism, however, which is expressed in the art of enticing people onto bold new paths, grows out of the ubiquitous dread that it may already be too late.

The reader will have guessed that this preliminary skirmishing is meant to forestall the inevitable awkwardness that arises when, after

125

the first doom-laden thunderbolt from on high, the mountain finally heaves and a little mouse of hope becomes due.

The model of civil labour

Civil labour presupposes civil rights, and it is also true that, through civil labour that can and must be done for others, civil rights pass beyond paper texts to become a palpable social reality in people's lives. It may be, then, that in a country where civil rights have developed only weakly or not at all, civil labour may have the function of making civil rights a practical reality, which may then spread to people's everyday existence and community life, but also to legislation, parties and politics. Civil labour is more than the commitment or engagement frequently invoked in relation to civil society, for it places at the centre of things the art of activity and becoming active – including the resources of time, space, money and cooperation necessary for that purpose. Unlike forms of voluntary commitment that acquire their status from being done without payment, civil labour is not paid work but it is rewarded with civic money and thereby socially recognized and valued. In the money society, money is simply the measure of all things. Civic money means a quantity for getting by with that at least matches the level of income support.

But there is more at issue. Civil labour should, as far as possible, be freed from worries about daily bread and personal future. And it should take the sting out of the growth orientation. The French head of government, Lionel Jospin, has characterized third-way politics as: 'market economy, yes, market society, no'. In this sense, civil labour is part of a state-approved exit from the market. Space is opened here for democratic society as citizens give their own chosen form to themselves.

Once again: 'Volunteering is not for free!' So who should pay? One source of civic money could be the huge sums spent in Europe on unemployment benefit and income support so that large numbers of people do nothing. Civil labour does away with this senseless arrangement, according to the slogan: Fund civil labour not unemployment! Recipients of civic money are not unemployed: they perform publicly important and effective civil labour, and for this reason are entitled to draw civic money. This would consist of public transfer money, social sponsoring by companies, local authority revenue (paid for things urgently needed by the community), as well as sums obtained from the civil labour itself. As the British example shows, quite considerable funds may thus be generated to support the material independence of this kind of 'political' labour.[94]

Civil labour, then, stands out from very many formless and non-binding types of 'civic engagement'. Alongside paid work, it constitutes an alternative source of activity and identity which not only gives people satisfaction, but also creates cohesion in individualized society by breathing life into everyday democracy.

The usefulness of civil labour does not lie only in the usefulness of the labour itself. There are also the social meaning and cohesion which, to a radical way of thinking, result from the failure of isolated individual projects. Community life becomes more colourful and controversial, involving a more substantial exercise of political freedom. None of the great influential thinkers – from Jean-Jacques Rousseau to Jürgen Habermas – ever wanted a democracy that exhausted itself in periodic elections. They all thought that it must include education, real democratic experiences, civic consciousness, and an alert and active community life – all of which are revivified and strengthened by civil labour.

Civil labour should by no means be confused with the pressure being put everywhere on benefit claimants to undertake work in the community. Civil labour is voluntary, self-organized labour, where what should be done, and how it should be done, are in the hands of those who actually do it. The democratic spirit that animates civil labour, and with it the society of self-active individuals, will perish if one commits the centuries-old mistake of confusing it with compulsory labour. The political character of civil labour requires public support and esteem for the independence expressed in autonomous, voluntary participation and organization. Of course, this does not exclude but explicitly includes cooperative structures and modes of insertion into the political life of the community – for example, through a civil labour committee that might advise on projects and help to enlist the necessary public backing for them.

Civil labour is also, wherever eyes flash and people act, a concrete labour of criticism and protest. It takes up issues that have been neglected, bungled or suppressed by administrators and politicians.

In particular, civil labour espouses the civil rights of minorities and the excluded, according to the motto: Tell me how the rights of minorities, outcasts and foreigners are handled in your country (by the authorities, in everyday life and the mass media, at pub tables, in your own neighbourhood, at night and in broad daylight), and I will tell you how democracy is faring in your country! Relative independence, free choice and basic public funding are the backbone of democratic culture, which civil labour can flesh out with substantive content.

Civil labour is not (only) a nice stopgap; it is not an institutional fig-leaf for government neglect. It mobilizes and integrates people as well as protest movements, and thus helps administrations, parties and the state to get up and running. After all, who first put on the agenda the issues of self-threatening civilization that are today on everyone's lips, and did so against the resistance of the ruling powers in politics, the economy and academia? The many David-versus-Goliath movements! And yet, civil labour also serves to defuse protest potential, turns it into pragmatic activity and self-activity, confronts verbal protest with the nitty-gritty of coming up with different initiatives and answering the question of what is to be done. Do not ask what the state can do, ask what you can do to eliminate the evils around us! With civil labour – to adapt something Schumpeter once said – creative disobedience supports a social site of recognized activity and experimentation. But one must avoid concluding that civil labour is the cradle of everything good and beautiful on earth. It can be either conservative or revolutionary – or both or neither. There is no evolutionary goal laid down in advance for the politically free society. On the contrary, the real litmus-test of freedom is the question: How are we to cope with the ugly aspects of freedom?

Civil labour has many other dilemmas to face. Let us mention just one. How shall spontaneity be organized? What must be done so that people leave their anonymous privacy and begin to do something publicly for others which does not bow to ready-made prescriptions or hierarchies? Everyone calls for spontaneity, creativity, innovation and individual responsibility, but no one knows how these big new (and initially empty) words of hope can be turned into achievable reality.

Over the past ten years the social sciences, especially in the English-speaking countries, have intensively concerned themselves with this subject and come upon what might be called the paradox of organized spontaneity. All attempts to make people happy by directing them to take organized responsibility for their lives – for example, by planning socially mixed housing areas, prescribing spaces for public activity, issuing guidelines for considerate social behaviour, etc. – are counter-productive. The more social spontaneity and responsibility are prescribed, the more they are hindered.

In legal-institutional terms, this means that civic labour should not be placed in the charge of local authorities, social welfare offices, labour exchanges, or even some newly formed civil labour department – not only because this would introduce counter-productive state control, but also because civil labour is supposed to strike a different note from the organized unimaginativeness of the local and national state. But this raises even more sharply the question of who will organize spontaneity.

It is a key idea of the civil labour model that entrepreneurship (in the original sense of the term) can and must be associated with work for the common good. We are talking of a public welfare entrepreneur, a kind of cross between Mother Teresa and Bill Gates. Social or public welfare entrepreneurs combine in their person that which appears to be excluded by the prevailing logic of functionally differentiated societies: namely, the application of entrepreneurial skills and talents for publicly useful ends. Welfare entrepreneurs organize memberships and work forms not exclusively but inclusively: civil labour shuts no one out, unless they shut themselves out. As experiences in Britain show, projects drawn up and implemented by public welfare entrepreneurs are often both more successful and less costly than parallel projects of the welfare state – because they are less bureaucratic and much more flexible in their organizational practices, and because they can draw upon a core of voluntary workers whose level of commitment could be purchased for a wage only with great difficulty, if at all.[95] Civil labour may thus become an innovation that permits other innovations. In so far as the welfare system is thereby given a new foundation, also in respect of content, it is at the same time decentralized and brought closer to real-life clients and problems. A culture of creativity takes shape – that is, a public space in which experimental diversity is possible.

The equipping of civil labour with an entrepreneurial sense of initiative throws up a variety of problems. How will this type of labour actually be funded? Who will authorize it, give advice and make sure that it serves public interests? And how will the failure – the bankruptcy, as it were – of certain projects be ascertained and handled? Civil labour also raises interface problems with regard to established players and forms of employment – problems such as a second labour market, community duties in a context of social work and other professional activity in the public sector, and the relationship to welfare associations, community service as an alternative to military service, retail services (with a low productivity), or work in the grey economy.

Some procedural expertise, such as we find practised in developed pluralist democracies, would seem to recommend itself for the tackling of these kinds of problem. Instead of substantive guidelines or demarcation criteria, a set of procedural rules would lay down how decisions were to be taken and possible frictions productively resolved. Such rules cannot be developed at the writing desk, however, but must be drafted, tested and legitimated within the democratic process.

How, then, can we sum up the meaning of civil labour? It is:

- organized, creative disobedience;
- self-determination and self-fulfilment in the form of voluntary political and social engagement;
- project-related, cooperative, self-organized labour for others, which is performed under the guidance of a public welfare entrepreneur.

As to the matter of civic money, the following points should be made.

- Civil labour is not paid, but is rewarded both materially and non-materially through civic money, qualifications, pension entitlement and 'favour credits' (for example, entitling someone engaged in civil labour to send their child to a creche free of charge).
- Civic money materially ensures the autonomy of civil labour. Its minimum level is derived from the standards of unemployment benefit and income support. It is added to out of community funds and resources generated through the civil labour itself.

Other things being equal, however, those who draw civic money are not recipients of unemployment benefit or income support, since they are active in publicly useful voluntary initiatives. Nor do they make themselves available on the labour market, unless they wish to do so. They are not unemployed.

But what does civil labour have to do with the founding of a world civil society in Europe?

The Europe of civil labour

The infinitely profuse and varied initiatives, organizations, networks and actors roaming the sphere that has come to be known as 'global civil society' have enjoyed growing attention in recent years. But this should not obscure the fact that all these Greenpeaces, Amnesty Internationals and the like are, so to speak, fine-weather birds whose public presence and political influence always seem to dissolve when things get serious. In the hard-boiled realist conception of political power, they therefore enjoy the dubious reputation – as does global civil society in general – of being a blown-up phenomenon at some remove from the national centres of power that decide on any really serious matters.

Even this sceptical view, however, has to confront the fact that the initiatives and actors of civil society play a key role in more and more public debates that influence the market and politics, on such issues as sustainable development, peace, minority rights and technological dangers, to name but a few. Citizens' action groups build their power by emulating big corporations. They form networks across frontiers and continents; they can be present both here and there at the same time, engaging in multi-locational power play in direct cooperation with government ministers and officials. If political influence is measured *inter alia* by the recognition which these civil society groups receive from formal political actors within national states and transnational organizations such as the United Nations, then it is possible to speak of the growing potential power of global civil society.

The Civil Society International

During the latest round of UN-sponsored intergovernmental conferences on the environment (Rio), human rights (Vienna), social development (Copenhagen), population policy (Cairo), women (Beijing) and urban habitats (Istanbul), tens of thousands of people attended the parallel forums of civil society organizations (CSOs). The practical and detailed knowledge of CSOs has made these forums a valuable resource for government actors.[96]

Furthermore, actors in the Civil Society International managed to gain some say over the agendas and events at these conferences, so much so that they have often taken part in the work of the governmental preparatory committees. They have, as former UN general secretary Boutros Boutros-Ghali once said, 'become an essential form of representation in today's world. Their involvement in international relations guarantees the political legitimacy of these international organizations.'

These initiatives and networks operate in a remarkable intermediate field. Whereas public opinion continues to be largely nationally oriented on a mutually excluding basis, the actors of civil society have long been transnationally organized to a degree that recalls the operations of the world economy. As individual states are forced into transnational cooperation through globalization in all its dimensions, the actors of civil society present themselves not only as major partners for national politicians but as pioneers of a transnational subpolitics. This also works itself out in multiple contradictions between the continuing ties of politicians to national states and their wish and compulsion to cooperate transnationally – contradictions which the actors of civil society can exploit to maximize their influence.

Let us be more specific. In the wake of globalization, the democratic states of the West develop a growing interest in transnational cooperation, because their most primal 'national' interests – beef, finance markets, cars, for example – within the world market as well as the labour market depend in quite basic ways upon how the definition and regulation of risks are negotiated in the sphere of transnational cooperation. Global risks, global markets, global politics, local jobs and local ballots are all directly linked to one another. National governments should really turn themselves into transnational actors – that is, cancel and dissolve themselves – if they wish to continue pursuing their national interests. But as they are famously unable to do this, they have to rely more than ever upon NGOs as pioneers rushing on ahead to solve national problems which are no longer national at all.

According to Martin Köhler, democratic states caught in this dilemma have two options open to them. Either they reject a strategy of cooperation and take flight in one variant or another of protectionist politics; or else they embark, 'through cooperation, on a long-term process of democratization of the external environment to obtain better conditions for the resolution of tensions and conflicts'.[97] In other words, the contradictions of national politics in the global age favour the construction of a cosmopolitan civil society, and this opportunity presents itself most especially in Europe.

Still, practical reliance should not be confused with purposive agreement. Whereas national governments look to 'Fortress Europe' as the answer, human rights groups, Greens and liberals try to save what can be saved so that their goal of 'Refuge Europe' is not completely abandoned. But often the only remaining question is how open a concrete wall can be.

> Refuge or fortress – this basic question has long been decided for Europe. Many EU states, acting partly for themselves and partly in concert, have bolted all the doors and windows. External border controls were brought into line by the Schengen accord and asylum procedures were regulated by the Dublin agreement. Germany has introduced an express procedure at German airports for asylum-seekers and drawn a safety harness around itself called the third-country rule. This is the centrepiece of its policy of self-insulation, whereby no one has any claim to asylum if they enter Germany from a country belonging to the EU or from one that has been officially declared to be safe; in such situations, they are simply sent back there. The third-country rule is becoming standard practice. All countries that are trying to join the EU want to conclude so-called security agreements: Poland with Ukraine, the Czech Republic with Slovakia, Hungary with Romania.[98]

Fortress policies, too, have to rely upon international cooperation. In Brussels, the protectionist reflex uses a military language which makes people forget that Europe is not threatened by enemies or criminals, and that other human beings are looking to Europe, the land where human rights originated, for the protection of their own human rights. Is the situation not favourable in Europe, then, for a human rights movement? But when before in history – in the anti-slavery campaigns or the black struggle in the United States – did a human rights movement initially have the legal protection it was seeking to achieve?

The foreigner and European identity

There is a lot of malicious talk about the Europe of merchants, the Europe of bureaucrats. Whatever wrongs or absurdities appear in the media are automatically attributed to the Brussels bureaucracy: it was recently reported, for example, that guidelines had been issued for the harmonization of Christmas trees, and that hunters will in future have to take a vet along when they go stalking. Be this as it may, there can be no disputing the fact that market Europe must urgently be supplemented and counterbalanced with a citizens' Europe. The stronger the euro becomes, the more it will need a counterweight. What could that be? What could become the soul of European democracy, of European identity?

Of course, a lot is at issue here. For Milan Kundera, the novel is the symbol of Europe: it echoes the laughter of the gods at the vagaries and confusion of a humanity deserted by the truth; the essence of Europe lies in its celebration of ambivalence, its irony and self-mockery. Similarly, it might be argued that theatre or music embodies the European identity. Perhaps a European constitution will one day create the Europe for which people strive. But it will not achieve that if it remains no more than a constitution, if it does not go together with a real understanding and practice of civil rights in Europe. A citizens' Europe will emerge only in a Europe of civil labour. There is no better way of breathing life into civil rights than to convert them, through civil labour, into the self-organized action of the sovereign Many.

My vision is of a European democracy that wins its soul through civil labour.

Let one example (but not a random one!) stand for many. The contradiction in which national governments have landed in the action contexts of world society is especially palpable in the treatment of refugees and immigrants. It is precisely these citizens of nowhere who are the first, exemplary citizens of world society. On the one hand, states want to seal themselves off from them; on the other hand, they are forced into transnational cooperation simply to implement their protectionist policies. Groups of citizens who are transnationally active on behalf of refugees are able to utilize this contradiction. The most promising halfway house between international community and national state is the regional level, and here the European Union offers citizens' groups good opportunities to establish themselves. These are based on the fact that Europe, an unfamiliar political entity, is developing as a unit with boundaries that are not yet fixed. Not only are relations among member-states – especially with regard to European civil rights – still not completely determined; external relations (association agreements, for example) are also ambivalent and susceptible to further definition; and member-states express different and often contradictory views about aspects of a common European policy on foreign affairs, internal affairs, security, the environment, social or labour issues.

The special opportunities to develop effective citizens' groups and civic labour in Europe, organized locally and active transnationally, result from the peculiar openness of the present situation. European civil rights constitute an appeal to shake up and redefine the relationship to foreigners within the European Union and among member-states. It may even be said that the definition of a foreigner is becoming the key issue of Europe's political identity. With the weakening of national demarcation, an Italian or Portuguese who used to become a foreigner on passing across the old frontiers must now be recognized everywhere as a European and be made at home legally and politically. The citizens' Europe becomes a reality only to the extent that mutual definitions of foreignness cease to apply among European member-states, so that people who used to be considered foreign are now looked upon and treated as the same – including, most especially, in cross-frontier (sub)political initiatives and networks.

Nowhere is this more striking than in the explicit concern of transnational civil movements and civil labour with ostensible foreigners. In the new Eastern states of the German Federal Republic, violence against foreigners has become an almost daily occurrence, without being decisively branded as an outrage by the middle layer of society or combated with all the available means of political enlightenment. A democratic awareness that one's own life directly depends upon public interests is only dimly present among many (especially young) people. Nazi slogans and symbols are even considered 'fashionable' and 'progressive'. Why, then, should a European civil rights movement on the basis of civil labour not be founded by East German groups in and for the new federal states, so that democratic culture develops self-actively through 'learning by doing'? Would this not, alongside the extra financial efforts, be an equally important contribution to the 'inner unity of Germany', and even more to the integration of the new federal states into democratic Europe? Some three millennia ago, it was in Europe that the idea of civil rights and political freedom, of *politeia* and *res publica*, first began its halting and stumbling triumphal march. Today this same continent can win its political identity only by redefining its relationship with foreigners.

Pierre Hassner, taking this one step further, proposes that European civil rights should be extended beyond the EU member-states to all Europeans who do not, or no longer, call their own any territorial state in whose framework European civil rights would equally apply to them. Romany interest groups, for example, have claimed direct access for their people to European basic rights. Should this not similarly apply to European refugees, who would thus find a home in a community that they would not otherwise have? The EU might then play the same role for persecuted Europeans that Israel has played for the Jewish diaspora. 'Would this not be the best demonstration that the future of European integration does not lie with Fortress Europe?'[99]

Concerned people and the ruins of socialism

If one wished to parody the civil labour vision, one might do this in the form of a song whose individual verses varied the crisis theme of the age – crisis of politics, crisis of democracy, crisis of values, crisis of community, crisis of crisis – and whose refrain promised each time: 'That's why we need civil labour!'

But joking aside, it is a question not of answers but of *beginnings*. Civil labour puts on a permanent footing a politics of new beginnings which, in opposition to the false certainty of hopelessness and failure – as Hannah Arendt put it – assumes that the capacity to start something new is an essential part of political action. This may be illustrated by an endless number of cases which derive their persuasive power from a concern with detail, and whose intensity and diversity are by no means exhausted in the relations of a European civil rights movement with foreigners.

Dörte Klages is one of those who are concerned:

I have been working as a grassroots volunteer for the last thirteen years. I first began in Heidelberg with the integration of people of no fixed abode, as they were called in those days. Nowadays one speaks rather of the homeless. The model we developed out of our work has really proved itself. Over these long years of work, I have learnt a great deal about why someone drops out of the system and why it is so terribly difficult – if not completely impossible – to get back in once you have landed on the streets. As a matter of fact, 95 per cent of people living on the streets want to be fully integrated and to be taken back into the community as unobtrusive citizens. But they will not do it alone; they need help. Here a psychological aspect is very important. The people in question are extremely reluctant to have anything to do with any official body. They are required to fill in forms at all manner of offices – social welfare office, job centre, health insurance fund, address registration bureau – and often enough they are quite incapable of doing this. There are hardly any social advisers who can help them – at most a few volunteers. This is where our organization comes in, by accompanying people to various offices and helping them to fill in forms. . . . By now there has been a lasting change in the attitude and behaviour of officials as a result of my initiative. Thirteen years ago I found accommodation for the first three – completely neglected – people without any abode, and within six months the number had risen to fifty-four. They are reintegrated fairly quickly (occasionally from one day to the next), as long as you get things right. Homeless people get housing only if they can show a rental contract from previous accommodation, but being homeless they do not have one in their possession. Then I was told by the social welfare office: But we would pay the rent – after all, we do have the best social system in the world. . . .

I think that civil labour could be extraordinarily effective in our society and could help save the state a lot of money, some of which is today senselessly squandered.[100]

Our society would do itself a favour if more concerned people had suitable structures in which they could become active – for whatever reason. For example, ecological initiatives – of which there are hundreds in Berlin alone – are often driven not so much by fear of destruction and collapse as by anger that most people do not think twice about the things they do. But the active rebellion against indifference has many other targets and aspects: work with old people, the disabled, AIDS sufferers and illiterates; practical familiarization with information technology; the invention of new ways to reduce energy consumption; the criticism of 'Frankenstein foods', and so on.

Are these all phenomena of the colourful urban milieux which, in the old states of the Federal Republic, had more than twenty years in which to practise intervention? No, there are many signs that Eastern Germany too is making the leap into civil society. A twofold aversion to the Western 'me first' and 'push and shove' society and to the state – both stemming from the experience of the GDR – provides a good springboard. Local authorities have to be careful, since citizens' anger at specific shortcomings can suddenly put them under considerable pressure. Publicly useful networks may be built up by Western foundations, often in association with local and regional authorities.

> In the depressed little textile town of Oberlungwitz, young people have dragged themselves off the streets and set up a youth centre. In Dreiländereck-an-der-Neisse, half a dozen action groups close to the grassroots are trying hard to gain the support of the local population. For five years, the State of Saxony has been helping the 'Action 55' group to carry out voluntary work among the long-term unemployed: low-skilled people over 55 years of age and with health problems.[101]

And back in the West, many lawyers, tax advisers, managers, skilled administrators, and so on are trying to use their abilities for something different – to influence public opinion and legislation, to draw up economic projects for self-help groups, to show how tax avoidance operates, to give advice to people saddled with debt, to uncover dangers that have been swept under the carpet, and so on. Community involvement and decentralization – a miniature cultural revolution has broken out in many local areas. What it promises is no longer just economic efficiency, but also increased democracy. 'All this citizens' stuff is only leading to parallel councils', complains one town councillor.

That is precisely the point. The appetite for democracy comes with eating.

Who is participating?

What are the real opportunities for voluntary civil labour? Is it not just an insignificant marginal phenomenon?

Let us look for a moment much further west. In the United States, citizens use their leisure time on an impressive scale to support public and social causes. In a Gallup poll conducted in 1990, 54 per cent of respondents said that they gave up four hours a week on average. In West Germany, by comparison, nearly a third of the population or 16 million people reported some voluntary commitment in 1994. And despite all the laments about the 'me first' society and the collapse of values, rates of engagement have actually increased since the 1980s. Nevertheless, individualization has its effect here too, in the kinds of engagement. Regular, bureaucratically organized 'voluntary work' for third parties has been decreasing, as otherwise willing people are often put off by the use of community service sentencing by the courts, while professionals keep the more appealing tasks for themselves. There is a lot to suggest that the decline in formal engagement should be interpreted not as a sign of spreading indifference and egoism but, on the contrary, as signalling a new kind of commitment against a background of individualization: more short-term, more specific, more deliberate but also more cooperative – therefore tied to particular projects that make sense, and create sense, in the volunteer's own life.

If one looks more closely at the sort of people who make a commitment to others, it becomes clear that 'biographical passages' are especially significant moments – unemployed academics and the new 'active' older generation being good examples. Couples with children tend to make the strongest commitment, while self-employed people tend to do the least.

What leads people to make a voluntary engagement? Here some distinctions are necessary. People in biographical transition – young people before vocational training, mothers after the child-rearing phase, older people who are leaving or have left paid work – want to be active on certain issues and in relation to a particular situation. Among the unemployed, they are principally young academics who are continuing their network and project work or committing themselves to further training. Young people want to do something community-based for two main reasons: they want to do something different from what they have done at school or in a company; and they want to use their talents in pursuit of an attainable objective.

The new demands on voluntary work relate both to content and to communication and cooperation. The engagement is expected to satisfy important requirements. It should be enjoyable but also demanding. It should be communicative, yield visible and calculable results, and bring about social recognition. New types of organization such as senior citizens' associations and barter rings point in the direction of civil labour. Voluntary engagement requires more free space, clear activity profiles, and a sharper definition of projects and group association. A new form is necessary to mobilize these independent motives and energies: the form of civil labour. Without it, the 'facilitating structures' will not exist to help bring about local 'supply structures' for voluntary social engagement. Civil labour means that it is no longer just the labour market but also political life which integrates people into society, by offering (limited) material security, esteem and identity.

Working citizens and civil labour

Civil labour must, however, be coordinated and inserted into a certain social architecture. How were the work society and democracy, employee status and citizenship, related to each other in the past, and how will they be related in the future? The first modernity was dominated by the figure of the working citizen, with the emphasis on 'work' rather than 'citizen'. For social recognition and integration were derived from employee status. Everything was linked to a paid job: income, esteem, security in old age, and so on. Paid work was thus the eye of the needle through which everyone had to be threaded if he or she was to become a full-blown citizen in society. Citizenship was a derivative status: it did not by itself enable people to make a living or to gain social recognition. The sequence of work [*Arbeit*] and citizen [*Bürger*] in the concept of the working citizen [*Arbeitsbürger*] expressed this clearly enough; it was the opposite of the word sequence in the concept of civil labour [*Bürgerarbeit*]. Only on special occasions was this working citizen also publicly something else – a voting citizen, for example.

This figure of the also-a-citizen integrated through work corresponded to a definite social architecture: the only addresses and actors of politics were the democratic state and the institutions (political parties, parliament) which played some role in formation of public opinion, decision-making and legitimation. Society, by contrast, was thought of as unpolitical – and many actually thought it modern and progressive that citizens should be relieved of the burden of political action in a democracy!

Life is acted out in the alternation between work and leisure. In other words, the active, providing state corresponds to a society that is active at work but otherwise largely passive. The dominance of a state-organized and state-monopolized politics also asserts itself vis-à-vis the economy and the market, although this is often disputed and not only by Marxists. To be sure, this model of 'employee society' (Lepsius) and 'working citizen' gained its persuasive power in Europe only after the Second World War, especially in contradistinction to the model of capitalist class society. The 'employee' refrains from any class-struggle rhetoric and receives instead a state-backed promise of rising living standards and social security. The citizen's political identity is thus given up at the workplace cloakroom.

If the diagnosis is correct that attractive forms of paid work are drying up, then this old social architecture must be losing its stability. Either one sticks 'even so' to the fiction of a full employment society and a politics based upon it – in which case, a Brazilianization of the West is what lies ahead. Or else a new harmony among state, political citizenship and market is developed and made the object of political debate and decision.

What are the tasks of a politics that must both abandon the state's role as all-round provider and facilitate the political society of active civil labour? How is politics to be understood and fashioned from now on, if national political actors have to rely upon networks of a transnational and post-national civil society in order to push through their interests? Can Europe ever achieve an everyday civic identity, if this does not emerge in projects of transnational civil labour? But what is the basis of legitimacy of the actions of such citizens' groups, which themselves by no means always embody pure democracy in their internal life (as has been rightly pointed out in criticism of Greenpeace's hierarchy)? How will it be possible to establish the society of political civil labour as a non-market society, at a time when the economy is extending its positions of power, in the form of global opportunities for action vis-à-vis political structures that are still territorially bound? How – and this is the question we shall now address – can and must we conceive of paid work and civil labour as coordinated in such a way that they do not, as it were, become two mutually antagonistic class spheres of future society?

Women's civil labour: not a way of being given the push

Women will be the first, women fear. The inclination to go out to work has been rising among West German women, and it has at least not been declining among East German women (90 per cent of whom had a job in the days of the GDR). So for women, is 'forwards to civil labour' just Orwellian Newspeak for 'back to charitable works', the latest way of pushing women out of an increasingly competitive labour market into activity from which no one can really make a living? Are they to be fobbed off with 'shadow wages' for odd jobs more in keeping with their biology: childcare, floor-sweeping or community welfare?

> The disjunction between the various shifts – in women's expectations, in the cooperation of the labour market and in the patterns of the home – is causing enormous concern. . . . On a political level there is little or no attempt to reconcile these tensions. One agenda exhorts us all to believe in the wonders of flexible labour markets, portfolio lives and transferable skills, while another howls about the destruction of the family and the need for more and better parenting. . . . The crucial interrelationships and inevitable contradictions between these two issues are rarely considered. The political rhetoric prefers not to see the possible inconsistencies.[102]

So, once again, rethinking and reorganizing the relationship between multiple work, time and money is the major challenge for a realistic policy of civil labour.

Gisela Notz lists the following conditions that will have to be fulfilled if a women's perspective is to be at the centre of civil labour:[103]

- a major cut in working time within the context of full employment;
- meaningful work that allows all who want it to earn a living;
- 'equality' of housework and outside carework with artistic, cultural and political civic labour in the voluntary sector;
- equal distribution among men and women of work that is (at present) paid and (at present) unpaid.

Once again, this raises the key question of how this model would be funded.

Animating democracy with civic money

The decisive step thus has two components. First, attractive forms of paid work must be distributed in such a way that everyone can have one foot in paid work and the other in family or civil labour. Second, the main point is to provide a financial underpinning for civil labour, so that people involved in it can through their own efforts consciously become at once partners and critics of the state. There are two ways of achieving this: either civic money fixed by law (not an arbitrary hand-out), or self-financing by private institutes. To detach social security from paid work and attach it to civil labour is the common import of the varying proposals that turn up here and there (whether the term they use is actually 'civil labour' or another one such as 'basic insurance' or 'negative tax'). In these ideas, the inalienable claim to a life worthy of human beings is associated not with the threadbare right to work but with citizen status and civic engagement. To attach civic money to civil labour means to reward political service. This new interpretation frees the state of its awkward responsibility for something that is beyond its capacity to deliver; it no longer has to keep promising paid work for all when it is unable to fulfil the promise. With the basic funding of civil labour, however, it creates a direct source of legitimacy for itself.

Three advantages are commonly mentioned by writers making the case for civic money:

- Facilitation of a low-wage sector, thereby combating long-term unemployment among the low-skilled losers of globalization.
- Prevention of income-poverty in general, encouragement of time out for further education, civil labour, etc.
- Reduction of the poverty bureaucracy.[104]

Often the plea for a guaranteed basic income or civic money is linked to the aim of freeing the poor from their poverty. This is doubtless an important and honourable aim, but on closer scrutiny it has more to do with 'crisis management', with pushing the poverty rate, like the crime rate, below a certain critical threshold, so that 'order' is maintained in society and politicians can present themselves at elections as effective operators. My own argument, by contrast, is that only civic money makes it possible to attain the republican ideal of a self-active civil society responsible for its own affairs. It is thus a self-grounding act of political society and not a hand-out to the poor; it allows society to give itself a new material foundation, as it were, and to gain a new political creativity.

Civic money should establish the conditions in which democracy can be given new life, and can be acted out in people's lives, where there is no longer full employment. It creates the minimum security required to make the insecurity of freedom productive. Civic money thus expands political freedom and fosters political individualism and republicanism – only thus does it become possible to tackle the great issues of the second modernity in a conscious and pragmatic manner.

Freedom includes lack of fear. Fearlessness grows and becomes stronger only where people have a roof over their head and know where their food will come from tomorrow and in old age. It is thus necessary to distinguish between two ways of motivating civic money: one is a circular self-justification in terms of the morality of concern for people in general, and especially for the slow, weak and different; the other is the material self-justification of political society according to which civic money allows the promise of the constitution to be practically fulfilled in everyday democracy.

But is it not contradictory to pin one's hopes on the state for the funding of self-active civil labour? What options are open for its self-financing? These are some of the possibilities in the United States:

It is an event organized by 'The United Way', a fund-raising organization of a kind which, despite some respectable efforts, does not exist even approximately in Germany. In the framework of a workplace gathering, the citizens' organization 'The United Way' presents ten projects in the fields of youth, culture and social questions. Then the company head comes to the microphone and announces: 'If you want to, you can put a cross against one of these projects on a printed form and enter the amount of your donation. For each dollar you donate, the company will double the contribution up to a maximum of 50 dollars a month for each donor.' In this way, $105,000 were collected in a company with a thousand employees. This means that an average of $4.50 a month was donated, which the company then doubled. In Chicago more than $100 million – in both the private and public sector – are raised for projects every year through such employee collections. . . .

In Germany there are currently two models. The Bertelsmann Foundation in Gütersloh is behind one of them. It has put up DM2 million of its own and called upon citizens and firms in the town to help it create a strong foundation. In a very short time some DM 4–5 million have been collected in this way.

The other model stems from the Hanover City Foundation. No one there put up a lot of starting capital, but around fifty citizens have pooled their resources: some donate money, others make their time available to develop ideas for projects.[105]

Switching between paid work and civil labour

It is crucially important that working time should be evenly reduced and a new (gender-neutral!) division of labour introduced for all activities in society, including housework. Civil labour is not a substitute for paid work but an important complement to it, which institutes a new identity out of self-activity for others. Civil labour is not an employment programme for the unemployed, but it can help them to find a way into the labour market. One crucial question is how paid work and civil labour can and must be opened up to each other (including legally), so that it becomes normal to switch between the two spheres of activity without incurring any substantial material loss. For state policy, on the other hand, civil labour may perhaps even allow a squaring of the circle: that is, a reduction in unemployment with smaller earnings and a rising demand for labour, in so far as new, meaningful, self-determined civic jobs have basic funding allocated directly to citizens. How could this work? Only in this way would it be possible for the state itself to create jobs at low cost: civil labour jobs.

The Dutch way

Here the promotion of part-time work reduces unemployment and transforms it into sovereignty over time. For this, however, two conditions that are not yet present in Germany would have to be fulfilled: old-age insurance for all, without any link to paid work; and social insurance cover for all employees, including those in cheap-rate jobs. Then and only then would the risks of labour flexibility no longer fall upon individuals. Perhaps in this way the 'miracle' of turning a shortage of work into time prosperity might actually come to pass.

> As long as part-time employees in Germany have to go with their eyes open into old-age poverty, there will be no redistribution of paid work through part-time arrangements. As long as a lot of low-skilled work can be shifted into the DM620 or DM520 temporary bracket, no sector will be able to develop there for regular part-time work.[106]

The Danish 'Time Out' model

The Danes successfully practise a model of redistribution that permits employees to take up to a year out for further education or child-rearing, to go on a long holiday or just laze around, or to engage in civil labour. The point is that during this period the voluntarily unemployed continue to receive substitute wages (the amount depending upon the reason for release), and of course also have the right to return to their job at the end.

> The Danes have thus created a means to relocate work-free time from the unemployed to those who, for whatever reason, want to have a period of free time at their disposal. Surveys indicate that 60 per cent of posts that become temporarily free in this way are occupied by the formerly unemployed. . . . The law is popular, because it allows for periods of further education and orientation, and because it considerably defuses conflicts between paid work and family labour that are hard to resolve for many young parents.[107]

'I'm a citizen-worker': bridges into the labour market

There is a widespread prejudice that, however valuable civil labour may be, it cannot help in any way to reduce unemployment. This is wrong for two reasons. First, it is often precisely unemployed people who help others and thereby themselves. Take the example of the 'Dresden Table' in Eastern Germany: 'Whereas elsewhere it is society ladies or municipal social workers who try to relieve poverty, here the helpers themselves come from the weaker section of society – unemployed and pensioners, students and convicted offenders. They all make a voluntary commitment. Even the woman in charge of the whole thing doesn't have a job.'[108]

Second, civil labour may well equip people for paid work. It imparts knowledge and skills which may also be documented in the form of references and testimonials. Why should someone who does well in civil labour not mention it as a major factor at a job interview? After all, 'I'm a citizen-worker' does sound better than 'I've been unemployed for three years.' Social pride and recognition through civil labour may break the stigma of unemployment and even turn it into its opposite. Why should personnel managers not prefer someone who has made something out of their unemployment by acquiring experience and new skills? Perhaps this sense of being useful is actually the most important 'qualification' that involvement in civil labour can provide. As the jobless assistant cook at the Dresden Table put it: 'This thing here proves to me that I'm still needed. It gives me a boost.'

Farewell to the monopoly on paid work

Unemployed people must, however, be allowed to commit themselves to civil labour without thereby losing their claim on the services of the Federal Labour Office. Hidden in this point is the need to reform the job support legislation – in the sense not only of opening it out to civil labour, but also of opening up the labour exchanges themselves so that they are no longer exclusively geared to paid work but also serve to promote civil labour.

The same applies to the incorporation of civil labour into social policy. A first small step to weaken the fixation on wage-labour is the recent German law on nursing care, which treats periods of nursing in the same way as child-rearing and allows them to count for pension purposes. When it is also (rightly) demanded that benefits should be funded out of general taxation in cases not covered by wage-labour, the question again arises of a tax-funded basic protection, instead of increases in central government subsidies for every occasion. Clearly a combination of part-time paid work and voluntary civil labour is less attractive in Germany than in the Netherlands, for example, where such a system of basic protection is already in place. Biographies in which combinations of paid work and civil labour do not become an economic burden are, in the given conditions in Germany, to be met with only among the affluent middle layers.

Three basic objections are heard to the easing of movement between paid work and civil labour.

1   Will the idea of civil labour as a complement to paid work not come unstuck on the egoism of our age?
2   Will people's identity not collapse in a workless society? How can transnational community ties be developed that are subjectively, culturally and politically sustainable?
3   Against the model of an experimental political society with cosmopolitan intent that takes active responsibility for itself – which has been presented here as an alternative to the

'working citizen' model – is it not the case that this would lead straight to a non-political society or indeed a society without politics, since democratic politics can ultimately be organized only within the framework of national states?

9

Vision of the Future II
Postnational Civil Society

Many will ask whether the above vision of multi-active citizens politically responsible for their own lives in an experimental democracy does not rest upon the idea that people are inherently good. Does it not repeat the mistake that appeared to have been finally laid to rest with the collapse of socialism? How can the formation of the self be linked to a living political society, in a way that does not merely substitute woolly fantasies for a harsh and cynical reality?

Everywhere there are growing fears that modern societies, which are highly pluralist and more and more split into opposing positions, are losing their capacity to develop common ties and value orientations. It may be objected that civil labour cannot counter dissolution of the socio-cultural biotope that first made it a possibility; that the model of hope which it offers is itself built upon the shifting sands of past idealisms.

The individualism of self-determined engagement

We are undoubtedly living in an anti-hierarchical age. The passage from traditional to industrial society went together with a passage from traditional (religiously grounded) hierarchies to political authority based upon bureaucratic rationality. But in this value shift, which began in the West but is no longer confined to it, concepts such as 'authority', 'centralization' or 'greatness' are generally subject to reservations; they are accepted less and less. In all the early industrialized countries, support for political leaders has been diminishing to an extent never before seen in the history of Western democracies. This can hardly be explained, however, by lesser competence on the part of heads of parties and governments. Rather, it expresses a fundamental change in value orientation and perceptual behaviour; the focus on values of individual self-fulfilment and responsibility has brought all hierarchies and their representatives into disrepute, quite regardless of what they may do or fail to do.

As Ronald Inglehart shows in a pioneering comparative study of forty-three countries with very different cultural backgrounds and levels of modernization, public political life is caught up in a process of structural transformation in all the industrially developed countries.[109] Everywhere it is increasingly likely that the public will act more autonomously of political controls, in a way that precisely challenges the role of political elites. One could, if one wanted to, say that citizens are becoming more rebellious, with the result that the authority and legitimacy of institutions are crumbling. Two lines of development that appear mutually exclusive – collapse of authority, growing intervention by citizens in politics – thus prove to be connected and complementary to each other.

In all the developed democracies, electoral participation has been stagnating or even declining; established political parties have been losing both votes and membership, sometimes to a quite dramatic degree. But anyone who concluded from this that there was growing political apathy would have completely misunderstood what is happening. For although voters and members are abandoning the old political oligarchies, they are not withdrawing into private life or nurturing political fatalism, but are involved more than ever before, in a wide range of activities that precisely criticize and challenge institutions and elites.

One finds everywhere that more education goes together with more activity in public life and politics; and also that younger age cohorts have been educated better and for a longer time than their parents were. Consequently, as the younger, better-educated cohorts gradually supplant the older, less-educated ones, we are likely to see a growth in active, self-determined engagement.

Many thus fail to recognize that, with the decay of social forms and orders based upon class, religious community or the traditional family, it is by no means necessarily the case that disintegration and anomie are stalking the land. The result is more an ethic of in-dividual self-fulfilment and responsibility, which is one of the most impressive achievements and sources of meaning in modern societies. Individuals who choose and decide for themselves, who are the self-staging authors of their own life and identity, are the most characteristic figures of our time. For more and more people, 'social progress' is measured by the extent to which opportunities are created for self-fulfilment in the value-references and dimensions of 'one's own life'. Helmut Klages shows from the example of Germany that it is this often-demonized individualism – and not the tradi-tional duty orientation! – which embodies a hitherto untapped source of engagement, a mighty 'social capital' lying dormant in both the eastern and western regions of German society.

This individualism should not be confused with consumerism. It is deeply moral. And at the same time it has a quite original social and political orientation. In many respects, we live in a much more moral age than the 1950s and 1960s. Today it is precisely young people who have often highly developed moral ideas about a wide range of issues – from environmental destruction, through the highly sensitive (and explosive!) question of partnership between the sexes, to healthy eating, human rights, ethnic minorities and world hunger. It is their very resistance to existing institutions which expresses this distinctively moral engagement of the (in many ways paradoxical) 'freedom's children', who have to come to terms with social security failures and deprivation at a time when expectations are still running high. This explains the crumbling allegiance to political parties, trade unions, churches, and so on.

For many people, especially the young, the argument that we must regain a sense of community through the old values and hierarchies sounds cynical, sentimental or morally two-faced. It cannot be stressed often enough that any attempt to create a new meaning for community and the public good – and thus to clear a way for the civic soul of European democracy – must start by recognizing the degree of the diversity, scepticism and individualism that are inscribed in our times and our culture. But let us listen again to the refrain that is already familiar to us. Civil labour is the decisive insti-tutional measure that integrates helpful individualists into social and

Vision of the Future II

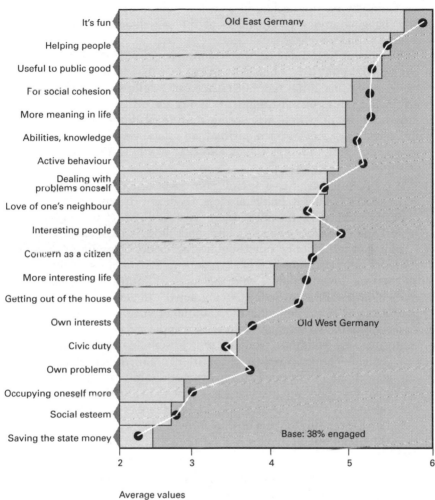

Figure 2 Reasons for engagement in the Federal Republic of Germany. What it means for people to make a voluntary engagement. *Source*: *Helmut Klages/Thomas Gensicke, Wertesurvey 1997.* © Campus Verlag.

political contexts of action and work grounded upon their own tenacity and initiative.

In fact, voluntary activity would today probably be in a very bad way if it entirely depended upon traditional virtues, for those virtues are undoubtedly on the decline in a society where values and attitudes are changing among the majority of the population, and especially among young people.

The surprising increase in voluntary unpaid engagement is explained, to put it in a nutshell, by the fact that such activity is not undermined and restricted, but rather powerfully supported, by the advancing values of self-fulfilment. Today too, of course, there are a large number of people who bring traditional duty-centred virtues into their voluntary engagement, and we can be very happy that they do so. Yet quite different things also play a role in the background motivation.

It is becoming clear that the differences between the old and new states of the Federal Republic are less significant than one might have expected. Crucially, however, there is a wide spectrum of values underlying people's engagement, and both traditional virtues ('helping others', 'doing something useful for the community', 'doing more for cohesion among people', 'practising love of one's neighbour') and self-fulfilment values ('enjoying oneself', 'using and developing one's abilities and knowledge', 'being active', 'meeting new people') play a major role. Alongside the traditional virtues that have been losing ground in society, new values have appeared in the background motivation of voluntary activity which stabilize and even boost engagement. The key message is that self-fulfilment values and civic engagement are not mutually exclusive but reinforce each other. Naturally we may find in particular cases that individualists are egoistic, but fortunately that is not the rule. Rather, there are a multiplicity of individualist reasons for this or that form of civic engagement – be it only the trivial one of 'having a good time'.[110]

The market and civil society in which we live encourage individuals to articulate their interests and to develop a sense of their individual specificity and responsibility for themselves. Now that we have so successfully achieved these goals – to an extent that our parents could never have dreamt of – the institutions are not there that would allow these highly individualized desires to be socially acted out and coordinated in the establishment of political interests and objectives.

It is precisely here that the civil labour model offers a key. It facilitates individualism in the shape of self-organization, independent initiative and experimental politics, but also in a form which matches the needs and demands of others (colleagues and beneficiaries). Civil labour may test out various models of 'active welfare', in which claimants are encouraged to assume greater responsibility for their own lives, and welfare itself is no longer measured in a sum of money or offered as a package of benefits. What is being tried instead is a concept and practice of welfare indissolubly bound up with greater self-control and self-confidence on the part of those who receive it. In this way, individualist culture may develop and put to the test a social ethic of its own.

The echo effects of transnational communities

But the key question remains. Where can transnational 'community ties' that are no longer supported by locality (neighbourhood), descent (family) or nation (state-organized citizens' solidarity) find their material basis and bonding power? How will postnational collectively binding decisions – that is, political action itself – be possible in the age of globalization?

The answer, which can here only be adumbrated, is at first intended to be not normative but empirical. I shall attempt, in a briefly sketched argument, to focus on the despatialization of social-political life and action, which has long been a normal part of everyday experience. The information and communication technologies, especially the integration of television into the perceptual horizon, influence people's image of themselves all around the world – as Joshua Meyrowitz, Arjun Appadurai, Roland Robertson, David J. Elkins, Martin Albrow, John Eade and many others have shown in complex theoretical and empirical studies. This has led to a situation where social communities, and political action based upon them, can no longer be understood from the point of view of a single location. In the debate about cultural and political globalization, a new 'grand narrative' thus seems to be taking shape concerning the despatialization of social and political organizations and identities.

It is often assumed that local communities are destroyed by cultural globalization, and that this makes it an Aunt Sally which hardly needs to be refuted. The real point, however, is that a locality is no longer the clearly demarcated system of communication that it once used to be. 'Today we do not rely in the same way as before on location as the source of information, experience, conversation, security and understanding.'[111] This also holds conversely for networking, social and political movements, which can eat up the distance of continents and generate proximity in real time – much as globally-locally active corporations do. The question at issue, then, is not at all whether communities are being lost or how they can be saved, but the fact that community formation in the global age has been 'released' from local ties. Social proximity, as the premise of a common existence and political action, can no longer be explained in terms of geographical proximity. There has been considerable discussion of the idea that human experience and action should be understood from the point of view of a 'generalized other place' (Mayrowitz). This means that the persons we experience as significant others are no longer restricted to those we know from direct encounters within a local community. Some persons, or perhaps even media-constructed and reproducible homunculi, serve people as mirrors of themselves.

Netwar

Political movements are discovering completely new ways of creating worldwide echo effects – including solidarity effects – as the central element in their local provocations. The violent local actions of the Zapatista guerrillas in Mexico during the 1990s, for example, cannot be understood simply in terms of what they physically did on the spot, but only if that is decoded as a means of gaining world attention and mobilizing national power. Mexico's Zapatistas, writes Castells, are 'the first informational guerrillas' to have made systematic use of the Internet and the new media as means towards their own political ends.[112] Rondfeldt, for his part, speaks of 'transnational netwar', as a new prototype of social movements in the global information age which has been tried out in Mexico.[113]

> The novelty in Mexico's political history was the turning of the question of who controls information against the political rulers, and this on the basis of alternative communications. The flow of public information that reached Mexican society was many times greater than what conventional communication strategies can achieve. Subcomandante Marcos gave his version as best he could, and the Church, the

journalists, the NGOs and intellectuals, but also the experts of financial and political capital, also gave their view of events. This abundance of opinions placed the social construction of reality in question. The vision of the ruling powers broke down.[114]

The sociologist Appadurai, whose research is devoted to transnational communities, writes:

All over the world, more and more people look at their own lives through the optic of possible ways of life offered in every conceivable way by the mass media. This means that imagination is now a social praxis; that, for many people in many societies, and in innumerable different variants, it has become the engine for the fashioning of public life.[115]

Imaginations that affect and arouse people, in which they spread out and evaluate their own lives, can no longer be deciphered in local terms. This does not at all necessarily mean that the world is a happier place. Rather, it implies that even the most mediocre or hopeless existence, even the most brutal and inhuman conditions, the worst experience or life of inequality, are today open to the play of an imagination produced by the mass media.

A 'global family': hate movements against globalization

'Anti-globalist' movements are also based upon, or play along with, the paradox that they use the *most recent* achievements of modernity, its communicative reach and resonance, to work toward objectives militantly *hostile* to modernity. They exploit the new world order, as it were, in order to make their resistance to the new world order as effective as possible. Perhaps this reference to militant anti-globalization movements will finally lay to rest the myth that civil movements in world risk society have got everything ' "good" and progressive' to themselves. William Pierce, the head of a militantly patriotic movement in the United States, writes:

In brief, the New World Order is a utopian system in which the US economy (along with the economy of every other nation) will be

157

'globalized'; the wage levels of all US and European workers will be brought down to those of workers in the Third World; national boundaries will for all practical purposes cease to exist; an increased flow of Third World immigrants into the United States and Europe will have produced a non-White majority everywhere in the formerly White areas of the world; an elite consisting of international financiers, the masters of mass media, and managers of multinational corporations will call the shots; and the United Nations peacekeeping forces will be used to keep anyone from opting out of the system.[116]

And for K. Stern:

The Internet was one of the major reasons the militia movement expanded faster than any hate group in history. The militia's lack of an organized centre was more than made up for by the instant communication and rumour potential of this new medium. Any militia member in remote Montana who had a computer and modem could be part of an entire worldwide network that shared his or her thoughts, aspirations, organizing strategies and fears – a global family.[117]

The Green self: the environmental movement has changed conceptual landscapes

By no means do I wish to ignore the fact that the power of transnational movements has its limits. Let us take the example of the worldwide environmental movement. With its actions designed to make people sit up and think, it has had an unparalleled career that has taken it from rags to riches; first demonized on all sides, finally a government party. In the 1990s some 80 per cent of Americans described themselves as 'environmentalists', and an equally large number of Europeans paid at least lip service to the goals of environmental protection. Every party and every candidate – wherever they stand and whatever they think – must behave in an 'ecologically correct' manner if they are not to end up in the political wilderness. This is not to say, of course, that their policies actually involve radical measures on the environment – often one has the impression of a tacit agreement between rulers and ruled to ensure the opposite. Transnational actors may also play virtuously with the contradictions that beset politics and the economy in world risk society, trying to win world public opinion over to their side, but for the moment they people the stage of real politics more as extras or as candidates for minor roles. The moment of truth arrives when, as in Germany in 1998, Green subpolitics is promoted to government policy.

The much-evoked national community is thus no longer the site of politics. Martin Albrow has shown that the collapse of communities in one place may not at all entail the collapse of community as such. Nowadays individuals orient and organize their links and networks much more translocally, even transcontinentally, so that anomie in one place may quite easily go together with living proximity in 'sociospheres' (Albrow) which, though still 'touching' the place, cannot be understood in terms of it.[118]

Let us repeat: there is a despatialized structure and organization of social and political life, whose 'logic', chances and dangers must first be set out and decoded. Someone who takes this direction will discover that forms of democratic decision-making, political organization, civil rights and civil labour can also be designed, developed and reconstructed transnationally. To make this clear, I should here like to distinguish three ideal types of active solidarity – family, paid employment (both of these in the framework of national-territorial solidarity) and transnational political community – and to do so in the three dimensions of work, care, and involvement in decision-making. The question, then, is the following. How are the division of labour, the distribution of care opportunities, and involvement in decision-making addressed or organized in each of the three types of solidarity?

The family: solidarity of inner space

Let us begin with the family type of solidarity. Forms in which the family is a specific organizational unit of work, care and decision-making are uncommon – and revealing. In contrast to paid employment, family work is aimed at clearly defined others (members of the family) and their needs; it does not follow the market principle that relates service and return service to each other according to rules of (monetary) equivalence, but makes possible non-equivalent forms of service or even, at the outer limit, service without anything at all in return.

Here lie both the central problem and the great opportunity of this form of work. Within the family framework, care is assured for everyone as a matter of course, without the need for further insurance. In this sense, the family mode of labour and care may be seen as a form of solidarity in which the weak have a natural claim without having to provide anything in return. Active family solidarity may thus be decoded as an almost ideal possibility of balanced care, to the benefit of those whose own powers – whether because they are young, sick or old – are not adapted to survival of the fittest in the daily rat race at which 'flexible egoists' excel.

On the other hand, this means that family labour and family services may be very unequally distributed; and that individuals allocated to such duties may derive no rights from them, either inside or outside the family microcosm. Indeed, this division of tasks according to the anti-equivalence principle, with its 'natural' allocation of duties without rights, means that it is mostly women (as a social role definition) who become the dutiful beings without rights of their own – rights to self-fulfilment, space and time of their own, money of their own, and so on. The fact that nothing can be enforced in return constantly strengthens and confirms the 'naturalness' of an extremely hierarchical division of labour and authority. Conversely, the radically unequal, 'male' form of authority based upon doing-nothing, being-looked-after yet wanting-to-decide-everything may again and again come into play – even in the non-religious, highly individualized milieux of a West where the power of tradition is weak.

Whereas the market model, in which work and care are equalized in the form of paid employment, can be generalized to any number of persons or objects and to relations between complete strangers, the exact opposite is true on all points for the family form. The principle of non-equivalent, spontaneous balancing of needs cannot be generalized; it excludes anyone who does not belong to a narrow circle of social relations set in advance by kinship. Active caring is here equated with caring within the family, so that practical humanity is restricted to face-to-face relations within the inner space of the family and may readily go together with indifference or even violent hostility toward strangers. The demand to 'love thy neighbour' is taken literally within the family but not generalized into the Christian precept of 'loving everyone as thyself'. The suffering of other people's children is disregarded according to a strict and narrow distinction between inner and outer; someone else's suffering takes place outside one's own field of perception, and it is equally possible to feel either compassion towards it or a complete lack of interest or *Schadenfreude*.

To conclude this sketch of the family form of work and solidarity, it should be mentioned that it has traditionally been seen as (in Durkheim's sense of the word) 'mechanical' – that is, it practises a collective solidarity in which individualizations are possible in only a very limited degree. Personal fulfilment or role and identity swaps – going to bed a Muslim and waking up a Catholic, to take an extreme example – point to a space of freedom that deeply contradicts the structure of family-ascribed roles. The other side of such anti-individualism, of the family form that is precisely not based upon exchangeability, contract and associated rights, is its cross-generational reliability. There at least, so long as the family clans exert power over their members' action and thinking, they also create lasting contexts of activity, obligation and care that pass beyond individuals or even generations. This applies less and less, however, to the family forms of the second modernity in conditions of individualization.

Paid employment: organizable solidarity

The question of how work, care and decision-making are related to one another in the schema of paid work may be directly counter-posed in every dimension to the family schema of solidarity. Paid work, being organized through the mediation of the market, involves service and return service according to (socially constructed) measures of equivalence, whose rules are (at least in formal employment) set out in a contract and therefore enforceable by legal action. The subject of labour and care is here not the family collective, but the individual 'freed' from it. Paid work therefore facilitates, but also compels, individualization, just as individualization presupposes paid work.

161

The solidarity of economically active individuals is thus in principle problematic. On the one hand, it still rests upon the tacit assumption of family care on which paid work itself supports itself. On the other hand, paid work defines a special area of social equality – whether through educational qualification (or the lack of it), place in the labour market, position in cooperative structures, workplace hierarchy, and so on. This horizon ties active solidarity to occupational definitions of inner and outer, limiting it and thus rendering it susceptible to organization. National or even transnational systems of initially specialist solidarity may (possibly!) arise. The expert is the transnational actor *par excellence*.

Though contrasted to family solidarity, this cross-frontier specialist equality should not be confused with social solidarity. It has, where things have worked out well, gained national acceptance, and it applies only anonymously, not in relation to specific individuals. It delineates social rights enforceable through legal action, and may thus also be instrumentalized in accordance with the principle of individual utility maximization (free-rider effect). Legal right takes the place of compassion and spontaneity. As a result, such solidarity tends to exclude the weak whom it is supposed to cover, whereas it favours the strong who have the knowledge and the leverage to assert their interests.

As to the dimension of involvement in decision-making, the labour contract assigns control over the goals of work to the 'purchaser' of human capacities; it is thus – politically – a contract of subordination. The goals, content and purposes of work are in the hands not of the workers themselves, but of those who organize the labour processes (usually in accordance with market principles). This does not exclude the negotiation of limited corporatist forms of control, mostly in connection with working conditions, workloads, forms of cooperation, and so on.

Transnational communities: solidarity until revoked

This brief sketch of how active solidarity is practised in family and workplace will serve to highlight, by comparison, the social form of active solidarity within transnational political community networks. It may be asked how modern societies – which dissolve everything pre-given, including the security of tradition and nature, and transform them into decisions – are able to cope with this self-produced insecurity. This brings us to a central invention of modern times: community-bonding through the sharing of risks. Risks permit individualization; they are related here and now to individual cases. At the same time, however, they yield an organizational schema of community construction and community ties that are capable of being formalized, in a way that separates them off from individual cases. This makes it possible to establish even mathematical probabilities and scenarios, as well as to negotiate norms for common rights and duties, costs and reciprocal payments.

In developed modernity there is no 'natural' community of neighbours, family or nation. There are only legends about their 'naturalness' (which can, of course, be extremely effective). The epithet 'natural' is quite deceptive, because it indicates forgetting or suppression of the fact that the 'natural' communities in question have been socially constructed or 'imagined' (Benedict Anderson). But what happens if the family withers as a basis of care and identity, if the combination of paid employment and national civic identity falls apart? The answer, is, perhaps, the development of risk communities.

The thesis I should now like to develop is that the risk regime also involves a hidden community-building power. If the states bordering the North Sea come to see themselves as a risk community in the face of constant threats from water, man, beast, tourism, capital or political mistrust, then this means that, over and above all national frontiers and trenches, a constructed and accepted definition of danger has led to a common area of values, responsibility and action which, like national areas, can create active solidarity among strangers. This is the case if the accepted definition of danger results in binding agreements and countermeasures. Accepted definition of risk thus establishes cultural value-horizons beyond national frontiers, and associates them with forms of more or less balanced, responsible and solidaristic counter-action. It answers transnationally the key question of active solidarity: If the worst comes to the worst, on whom can I rely and to whose aid should I come? Risk communities thus combine elements that appear to be mutually exclusive:

- They rest upon culturally shared values and perceptions.
- They can be chosen.
- They may be regulated either informally or contractually.
- They thus generate transnational, socially obligating proximity, within culturally shared, socially constructed risk definitions that stretch across frontiers.
- They are not all-embracing but relate to particular themes and priorities.
- They form a moral space of mutual cross-frontier obligations. This space is defined by answers to the questions: From whom can I expect help? Whom must I help if this or that happens? What kind of help should I expect to receive and give?

The realities perceived and assessed as risky are realities not of destiny but of civilization. Thus, risk communities do not have to be accepted as a fate; they are at bottom political communities, resting upon decisions and questions that may be addressed and answered in different ways. Who is responsible? What must be done and changed, in matters both big and small, to ensure that the threat does not materialize?

Risk communities are thus similar to family communities of responsibility. Unlike them, however, they are not compulsory communities: nothing is laid down or prescribed in advance. They do not rest upon narrow kinship definitions of inner and outer, but (may) cross boundaries to embrace few, many or perhaps even an unlimited number of definitions. Risk communities differ according to the answers they give to the questions: To whom are we responsible? For what and for whom? These answers are specified in a set of reciprocal relations.

It is true that I cannot protect myself against other life-threatening risks that might ensue (for example, from the building of a nuclear power station or a chemical plant not far across the border). But I decide how significant and relevant to action these will be for me – or whether, in the face of BSE, I keep my fondness for steak or convert to vegetarianism.

As risks are socially constructed and recognized as bound up with cultural values, but are also based upon (scientific) knowledge of technological possibilities and dangers and how these can be reduced, risk communities are inherently susceptible to controversy and have to withstand, integrate and balance a plurality of perspectives, questions and starting-points. They do not negate commonality, but they do have a positive attitude to differences. Their active solidarity is not given in advance, but must be continually strengthened across cultures, continents and opinions.

Global risk regulation: climate politics

The global environmental danger most discussed at present is climate change.[119] From the international interpretations of this major risk, in all its dimensions, side-effects, ambivalences and value-horizons, as well as from the related history of transnational agreements so full of hesitations and setbacks, one can study as in a picture book the integrating (or disintegrating) power of the risk regime. Scientific diagnosis, cultural assessment and political consequences are here directly interconnected. According to the explanation most favoured today ('construction'), trace gases are destroying the earth's thermal balance by partly blocking the radiation of heat into space. This means that the CO_2 risk is especially a North–South problem, since its level is strongly proportional to gross domestic product. Emissions of CH_4, on the other hand – which account for roughly 18 per cent of the greenhouse effect – are more of a South–North problem, in that large quantities of this gas are produced in agriculture in the countries of the South.

The depiction of consequences – the melting of polar ice, rising ocean levels, a threat to the third of the world's population living near sea coasts – brings into being a certain kind of global risk community. Through the Rio Earth Summit (1992) and the follow-up conference in Kyoto (1997), this global risk community seemed to become firmly established against all remaining doubts and doubters, in the sense that the roles of fringe and mainstream were reversed. Anyone who still questions the danger is an international outsider. At the same time, measures to regulate risk (cuts in emissions, schedules, obligations to report back, etc.) were made binding at mammoth sessions full of heat and drama. The task now, in designing more or less leaky strategies for a worldwide reduction in gases (and therefore in consumption opportunities and markets), is to enforce these norms against national egoisms without the central power of a world government. One can just discern here how risk communities are communities of responsibility, in which at least a start can be made in inducing national groups and actors to implement transnational priorities.

Networks of diversity: elaborate ways of handling contradictions

Territorial communities are generally multi-purpose or all-purpose communities. And they are 'congruent': that is, the frontiers and the radius within which their objectives apply are coextensive. It is precisely this which is not true of self-chosen risk communities. These form multiple networks which, instead of being subject to the Either-Or principle, complement and overlap one another – though not according to a single all-inclusive principle of value or governance, but in a manner that is despatialized, goal-specific yet morally obligating. The welfare state, too, may be decoded as a dialectical unity of risk community and insurance community.

These kinds of division of risk responsibility do not necessarily, yet may also, have an explicitly political stamp and organization. A good illustration of this are human rights and transnational women's networks.

As the last corner of the earth has been brought into the world market, women from all cultures and ethnic groups have confronted a global-patriarchal politics, while also retaining an impetus to organize resistance. Migration within and between regions has created 'mixed identities': people who live in and between several cultures and unite different influences within themselves. Instead of an artificially pre-established national solidarity, one sees appearing a multicultural plurality whose basic element is the different, the special, the distinctive. As far as politics is concerned, this means that the capacity to engage in politics on the international arena must be combined with references to global 'diversity' – a field of tension from which the feminism of the twenty-first century will draw its strength, but

166

which may also provide the stuff of controversy. Do political capacities on the global stage conflict with political and cultural diversity?[120]

Respect for diversity and self-help, as well as a solidarity which encourages, supports and assists, are principles that help many of these active networks to gain credibility and recognition in the eyes of the public – and in the eyes of democratic governments, which are also committed, constitutionally at least, to the same principles. The Indian feminist Kuma-D'Fouza speaks of 'unexpected combinations that become possible through dialogue under the paradigm of diversity'.[121] The very experience of the diversity, ambivalence and multilayeredness of the repressive relations that women endure (but in which they can also be complicit) sets up transnational commonalities and communities. 'Race, class, caste, sexuality, nationality, religion, everyday problems and handicaps – to name but a few – all play a role along with gender. The category "woman" alone does not do justice to this reality. Rather, many different feminisms, grouped as kaleidoscopic fragments around the category "woman"', should build common links, coalitions, and mutual support communities.

In this way, beyond all fragmentation and conflict, tried and tested transnational support networks are taking shape which do not fear or deny differences, but draw from them their credibility and even their national power. What is thereby acquired and practised is the activity of 'translation', in both the metaphorical and the literal sense of the term. The translator speaks more than one language, belongs to more than one world, experiences and suffers the false stereotyping of foreigners through which lifeworlds are sealed off from one another, and even from themselves. In everyday transnational existence, the act of 'translation' – the toing and froing among various orders and disorders – becomes a permanent balancing act, an elaborate handling of contradictions that often enough ends in failure. We are the experimental field out of which transnational civil society is taking shape! This is how networkers belonging to all cultures, colours, religions and political persuasions understand themselves.

Limits and strengths of
transnational civil labour

In contrast to family labour and paid work, even if transnational civil labour receives basic funding and draws civil money on a regular basis, it remains materially independent and geared to other sources of income. One result of this is that civil labour will never be in a position to supplant paid work, to the extent that paid work historically supplanted family-based labour. Oriented and organized in such a way as to complement rather than replace, it will remain limited to fields of activity that may not be perceived at all, or only inadequately, in the spheres of paid work and family labour.

But this has a major implication for the political content of civil labour. If paid work is, so to speak, a 'politically emasculated' form of praxis shaped by the employment contract, which in relation to workforce involvement in decision-making actually means something more like a rush to obedience, then civil labour is the exact opposite, since there is no direct leverage for the imposition of external control.

Paid work can be performed only where clients with enough money are prepared to pay for it. Family labour presupposes ascriptive membership of the small circle of the kinship group; rights do not come into it. Moreover, the goals of family labour (at least in the traditional forms present throughout the world) are based upon rigid authority relations that typically exclude any participation in decision-making. The situation is quite different in the case of voluntary, self-organized civil labour. Here the initiative in dealing with a particular problem – as well as the initial choice of the problem and goal of activity, and the type and methods of practical organization – cannot come from someone else but only from workers within the group itself. Here too it is the specific problem, the visible annoyance, the feeling of concern which are the forces impelling them to become active. A group which comes together more or less spontaneously, or which is mediated by a common problem or situation and its 'translation' across cultures, may take up in this form almost any problem that strikes it as pressing and important and tackle it in a way that seems appropriate. In the first stage, it needs no sponsor, no educational qualification, no master

168

craftsman's diploma, no rulebook, and not even the kind of official approval that is required to make a fire in the forest.

In other words, whereas in paid work (and also in political activity dependent upon an electoral mandate) non-workers such as donors, voters or party organizations supply a crucial impetus and have considerable scope for supervision and control, the relationship is exactly the opposite in the case of civil labour. Here the first initiative comes from the people now active on the issue; everyone else can exert only indirect influence over the work, and in the end only to the extent that the group itself 'authorizes' them to do so – unless, that is, the civil labour project is so expensive that it requires major external funding. Thus, citizens' action initiatives cannot be 'called into being' or 'voted out' by donors; no one can gain control of them by depriving their members of the means of subsistence or by threatening to drop them from the party list at the next election. The action exists for as long as its initiators commit the necessary time and energy and see it as a source of self-activity, self-affirmation and self-fulfilment (in the service of others).

One special feature of civil labour is that in the development of such forms of practical concern for others – precisely according to the principle of independent initiative – the appropriate forms and methods are not established in advance, but have to be created 'in unison' with the content and goals of the civic labour itself. The group's mode of working and functioning is not independent of the specific project; the structures of its activity are dictated not from outside, but by the goals that the group has set itself. The civil labour must therefore pull itself up out of nothing by its own efforts, and in the process generate its object of labour and its procedural and organizational methods. This, no doubt, is what makes it such a precarious and experimental form of political practice.

In citizens' action groups and transnational networks, the main point is often not to allocate certain duties to oneself, but rather to help others see, and encourage them to tackle, certain tasks and problems within their special area of competence. Thus civil labour, unlike paid work, does not tend to establish a monopoly over tasks, but often seeks to mobilize others whose inactivity, or erroneous or unjust practice, needs to be publicly exposed. Civil labour, then, may also be understood and organized as a mode of labour and a form of practice which stretches across, or runs parallel to, a number of rigidly defined administrative and political domains, competing with them as to content and criticizing and correcting them on the basis of what they are intended to achieve. It is precisely not based upon an exclusive division of labour (which may sometimes, in the case of paid work, lead to rivalries and demarcation problems).

Another strength of transnational networks and political movements is the fact that quite ordinary people around the world commit their surplus time and energy to a cause, on their own initiative and of their own free will. Usually these movements have neither money nor other resources in any great quantity. But they do have what institutional actors in politics, administration and the economy often lack: namely, cultural credibility. They engage in the pursuit of certain values, profiting from knowledge and abilities that are neither spoon-fed them by the state, private companies or religious leaders, nor necessarily used for private consumption.

Transnational movements are thus dependent upon certain conditions of production, consumption and labour of present-day capitalism, in so far as these promote the spread of new cultural practices and encourage new forms of identity.

> It is one of the contradictions of capitalism that, while operating within a state and relying on its support on key issues, it also puts up a fight against state regulation and constantly seeks to expand into new markets. This is true of cultural products as well as of all others. This is not to say that capitalism directly fosters global movements, but only that, as a result of processes meant to impose new styles and images which exploit the developed taste of skilled workers – which, in other words, are directed at the consumers and producers of culture-capitalism – it is no longer possible to control what individuals make of such possibilities. Workplace discipline no longer counts when workers make their consumption decisions. Because of the values held by consumers, capitalism must therefore bow to, or at least take account of, public opinion on matters relating to large-scale industrial projects, toxic emissions and widely rejected production technologies.[122]

Transnational civic movements may operate successfully, then, where consumer society and political engagement are on the same wavelength. They refute the simplistic notion of a homogeneity of interests between state and capital, because they represent a budding world citizenry that national governments cannot simply ignore. As

170

a number of examples clearly show – from various transnational shopping boycotts to the Greenpeace campaigns over the Brent Spar oil rig in June 1995 and the French atomic tests in the autumn of the same year – citizens' movements with a presence in the mass media are capable of entering the political arena as new players in conflicts and negotiations with the state and the economy. These non-governmental civil labour groups can thus flex their muscles on the world stage. But the idea that they 'can take over where government is failing . . . is fantasy. The nation-state and national government may be changing their form, but both retain a decisive importance in the present-day world.'[123]

The dilemma of democracy, or the unclear site of the political

But is not the move to a transnational social space therefore not an illusion – one that is non-political because undemocratic (and even dangerous to democracy)? For democratic legitimacy – many say and believe – is always ultimately possible only within the framework of the national state and its political arenas (parties, parliament, public life).

The answer has to be a clear and double 'no'. The site of the political has become unclear in the age of globalization, or at any rate the formally signposted jurisdictions and lines of communication no longer speak for themselves. This may be illustrated simply by asking what would happen if the EU applied to join the EU. Obviously it would be refused. For the EU does not meet the requirements of democracy that it has itself made a condition of membership. This may be taken further, moreover. Let us imagine that, a few weeks after the negative answer was given, the member-states of the EU were stunned to receive an announcement that the EU had regrettably been compelled to deprive them all of membership. Why? France, Germany, Britain and all the others no longer met the democratic criteria for EU membership, because more and more decisions were being taken autonomously by the EU and then merely implemented by the member-states.

This brings out well the democratic dilemma in the age of globalization. Whereas, in the democratically constituted framework of national politics, to persist in not making a decision is increasingly seen as a legitimate position, decisions are taken within the transnational framework of apparent 'non-politics' which, though far-reaching in their implications, lack any democratic legitimacy. This 'governing without government', as James Rosenau calls it, is as important in international organizations as it is democratically illegitimate.

Why, for example, was a Europe-wide referendum never held on the introduction of the euro? That would have spurred Europe on politically, by creating a European public realm and identity around a truly European matter.

A century and a half ago, during the 1848 revolution, there were heated debates in the Paulskirche in Frankfurt over the transformation of the religiously grounded feudal order into a nation-state democracy. Today we should be debating the transition from national to transnational or cosmopolitan democracy.

Looking back to the first modernity: the logic of institutionalized conflicts

The many competing modernities of the future will differ from one another on a number of points – for example, how they mediate between the values of community and freedom; whether they continue to think that heaven on earth can be built step by step out of technological innovations; or whether they accept technological change as inevitable but seek to tame it with democratic and ethical principles. Another question, perhaps the key one, will therefore be how consistently and in what forms they develop institutions of transnational conflict-regulation, and whether or how they confer upon these an autonomy and a rationality of their own.

In the first modernity, these problems were raised, argued over and converted into political routines in the arena of the national state. Above all, the conflicting sides were disarmed and obliged to limit themselves to discursive exchanges in parliament and public life. The state enforced its claim to a monopoly of violence and, at the same time, inaugurated the competition for political aims and consent within democratic institutions such as free elections, freedom of assembly, freedom to found political parties, a parliament with specific rights and duties, and so on. The institutionalization of conflict thus presupposed that social and political conflicts would be not demonized and suppressed, but *recognized*. The parties to the conflict, however, were obliged to refrain from violence and to fight it out with one another only within certain structures and procedures – ideally those of parliamentary democracy.

This idea of institutionalizing conflict also applied to the industrial class struggle between labour and capital. The early capitalist class society of the nineteenth century, which had been marked down by Marx's diagnosis for growing impoverishment or revolution, was tamed and civilized in so far as institutionalized forms of conflict resolution – above all, collective bargaining – were asserted right at the heart of the social conflicts of the labour movement. Trade unions and employers' associations, acting independently of the state, negotiated the terms of the labour contract according to a fixed agenda, upon the basis of figures for their sector of the economy. Even the right to strike or lock out was allowed to the other side, as long as certain procedures (a prior ballot, for example) were followed.

Here too the recognition of conflict, and its prescribed legal regulation, helped to ensure that necessary and sharply focused struggles would not endanger society but actually become the source of social and political renewal. It might well be said that the calculated passage from denial and demonization of social and political conflicts to their recognition within civilized procedures establishes a crucial yardstick for measuring the actual 'modernity' of ostensibly modern societies.

Looking forward to the second modernity: transnational conflict regulation

It can now be seen that a congenital defect of the first modernity, which will become a dramatic problem in the second modernity, was the fact that forms and procedures for the institutionalization of conflict were developed and deployed almost only within individual countries, and not where highly explosive areas of conflict will appear in the global age out of a mix of protectionist reactions, cooperative compulsions, and multidimensional issues calling at once for radical and clearly defined changes in economics, administration, politics and everyday life. Of course, in our world even the global and the transnational have their addresses and jurisdictions: the General Assembly of the United Nations, the Security Council, the International Court in The Hague, or – at European level – the supranational institutions of the EU. Yet it is not hard to prove the blatant disparity between, on the one hand, the new and ever sharper sources of conflict among nations, religions and cultures, and, on the other hand, the small number of rather toothless institutions for transnational or even global conflict resolution which somehow float in the stratosphere, as morally demanding as they are politically non-binding.

The old-new sources of conflict are easier to name than to exorcize. In the first place, the imposition of free world markets must be emphasized, for at least two reasons. Within national states where strong workers' parties have achieved social security systems and forms of union bargaining power, it is running into trouble with the deinstitutionalization of the conflict between labour and capital. The demand for 'flexibility' now on everyone's lips means nothing other than that the existing forms of regulation – collective labour contracts, workforce participation or safety standards – are up for renegotiation, and will be relaxed or discarded. At the same time, the neoliberal revolt aims to cut the state back to a minimum, both nationally and internationally. But this can easily turn around into a militarization of conflicts between and within individual states.

Here we can do no more than mention some other new sources of conflict, also quite unpredictable in their consequences: ecological crises, disasters and collapses (as a result of chemical or nuclear accidents, climate change or struggles over scarce resources important for survival); and the shadows cast by divergent modernities wrestling over fundamentalisms new or old.

As the world opens up and is forced closer together in the distanceless space of the mass media, as the modes of production and labour characteristic of transnational corporations stretch across frontiers and continents, other hard-to-assess sources of conflict result from the overlapping or combination of virtuality and reality. These include the global risks and dangers of migration from poorer to richer parts of the world; of nuclear power stations that may explode tomorrow or in a thousand years; of the silent and hidden new International of organized crime, and so on. It is characteristic of these global threats that, precisely at times and places where they

174

have not previously appeared, they may develop a power to change society which activates the underlying political meaning of the dramatization of risk: namely, the need to act before it is too late.

Quite fundamentally, the transnational conflicts that ensue from and flesh out the victory of neoliberal policies will mark the everyday course of economics, politics and people's lives. The last few years have witnessed the liberalization of a number of highly regulated industries: telecommunications, energy, food and finance. The resulting worldwide competition has brought various national standards agencies into conflict with one another. With the free trade in commodities, the problem has become global – but all this is just the beginning. Already further sources of conflict are taking shape, such as the regulation of the global environmental and labour markets, or even thornier fields where there is a high degree of political sensitivity.

The first wave of national deregulation has made necessary a second wave of transnational regulation. This enhances the value of that which was devalued in the 1980s: the state and politics. What is required is the exact opposite of neoliberal deconstruction: namely, strong states capable of transnational market regulation both within and beyond frontiers. To the extent that such arrangements are found, invented and negotiated, globality becomes a key theme and a pivotal issue of conflict – not only in politics and economics, but also in the daily lives of people around the world.

What follows from all this? In a world that has become smaller and more conflictual through the erosion of distance, the task of political action, using all possible human creativity and political-institutional imagination, is to create and test out, and make every effort to establish, transnational forums and forms of regulated (that is, recognized and non-violent) handling of mutually exclusive national, religious and cultural 'egoisms' often explicitly hostile to one another. This will not happen by itself – we can be sure of that. In order that this conception of transnational institutions and transnational recognition/handling of conflict – a conception at the core of cosmopolitan democracy – should acquire political shape and power, a new political subject must be founded out of cosmopolitan national movements and parties. To this end, transnationally active and oriented citizens' action groups, as well as civil labour contexts that remain to be created, can give a decisive impetus and develop practical foundations and workable models.

Cosmopolitans of the world, unite!

It would fall rather short of the mark simply to adopt the Lilliputian principle that a large number of minute political creatures can tie down the national giants. What is needed, rather, is to spell out anew the dual principle of conflict regulation: recognition of oppositions, differences and conflicts (with demilitarization and non-violence in both words and deeds); and the creation of legitimate sites and procedural techniques for the handling of conflicts. This raises a number of further questions.

First, and most important, where do such transnational experiments have a prospect of being successfully started? The answer has to be Europe. A return to nation-state democracy is purely illusory. There can no longer be any democracy in Europe unless it is transnationally expanded. Particularly after monetary union, Europe must be strengthened with new political ideas. For only a strong Europe will be in a position to absorb and overcome the already predictable social and political problems and the turbulence resulting from them. And only a strong Europe will be in a position to redefine its invention of politics for the global epoch, so that, for example, a Briton, Pole or Italian is able to intervene in a German election campaign because he or she is a member of a party present in every European country – and intervene because, in that campaign, European or global politics is being pursued under false (because purely national) labels.

There is also the question of the level of mediation. Where should conflicts be institutionalized – transnationally, globally, or nationally and locally? Are these different sites and levels mutually exclusive? The general lesson to be drawn from the experience of transnational movements is that activities at different levels complement and reinforce one another. But perhaps that is a lesson based upon the relative impotence of those movements, which no longer applies if the point is to force powerful national egoisms to compromise with one another. How, in that case, can the grand political objective of an institutionalization of transnational conflict be meticulously

176

translated into detailed action? What would 'collective bargaining' between Turks and Germans have to look like in Berlin, for it to allow conflictual perspectives on both sides to be effectively handled?

We *must* create and win public support for sites where fruitful encounter can take place. We *must* argue and struggle for the recognition and implementation of basic rights, gain the help of powerful new actors who can establish durable coalitions to achieve that goal. In this connection, Amnesty International recently approached major economic players (companies and banks) to gain their active support for the defence and promotion of human rights. At present, death sentences, torture, political imprisonment and other violations of civil and political human rights are seen as things that can be accepted, so long as they do not have an adverse effect on business. But it is well within the power of big corporations to put a stop to them – for example, by making respect for human rights an integral part of their decision to invest in a particular country. Such a change in company policy might produce credibility (and good publicity), which its whole advertising budget could never buy for it.

We *must* found transnational interest-groups and political parties, or reorient and reorganize existing ones. We *must* create formations which actively open up for transnational conflicts, issues and values the still mutually closed public and political arenas. Unless transnational conflict-regulation is tested in this way at the heart of the national organization of interests, the period ahead of us threatens to become a post-political one of high technocracy. The power and importance of such kinds of transnational network are based upon their capacity to uncover, make transparent and handle cultural-political oppositions and 'egoisms'. But they face huge difficulties both nationally and transnationally: already it seems scarcely possible, for example, to bridge the discord between the United States and the European Union over food safety issues; and such problems will increase where the clash is greater between the cultural backgrounds, income levels and political systems of the countries and regions concerned. Transnational or cosmopolitan parties must not only endure and handle such contradictions within themselves, but also gain the necessary political strength through identity-building conflicts *against* movements calling for renationalization. In other words, they must fight for and develop an

177

independent ethic and rationality of transnational conflict-regulation within each of the national-cultural milieux.

We *must* open up and practise the new power game of multilocal politics. Transnational civil movements and parties will then pull level with the corporations and break out of the territorial trap of national politics, by becoming active both over here and over there and thus playing off national states against one another. The watchword is: Learning from the economy means learning to win!

We *must* create new institutions for the handling of conflicts between states, and develop and test out mediators, arbitrators and possible procedures. But this means that there have to be cosmopolitan movements and parties of French, North American, Polish, German, Japanese, Chinese, South African and other provenances which, by interacting with one another in the various niches and perspectives of world society, struggle to bring about transnational institutions of conflict resolution.

That leaves one final question: Who are *we*? Who come into consideration as bearers of such a cosmopolitan civil movement? In those places where globality becomes an everyday problem or the object of cooperation – in the big global cities and the transnational organizations – the milieu and mentality of a self-conscious world citizenship take shape with a post-national understanding of politics, responsibility, the state, justice, art, science and public interchange. However, the extent to which this can already be seen as existing, or as likely in the future, is a completely open question both empirically and politically.[124]

Multiethnic world society should not, of course, be idealized. The appropriate metaphor is not so much a melting-pot as a crucible, where cultural identities rich in colour and conflict exist alongside and in opposition to one another[125] – and where not only tolerance and joy in diversity but also exclusion and xenophobia are able to grow. Such reactions do not prove at all that the multicultural experiment has failed, but they do indicate that appropriate forums and forms are not yet present for the regulation of conflict.

The work society is drawing to a close, as people are more and more replaced by smart technologies. Must this all lead to catastrophe? No, on the contrary: only when all passive toil at machines has been successfully done away with, will human creativity be free to answer in detail the great questions of the second modernity. Whether it will be done successfully or not, no one can say. So why should we only be either pessimistic or optimistic, and not both at once? For the question of whether a European cosmopolitan movement is capable of becoming reality can find an answer only where it belongs – in the practical space of politics.

This would then realize one of the main ideas of Kant's *Perpetual Peace*: 'To consider oneself, according to internal civil right, as an associate member of a cosmopolitan society is the most sublime idea anyone can have of their destination. One cannot think of it without enthusiasm.'[126]

Notes

1   W. Bridges, *Jobshift: How to Prosper in a World without Jobs*, London 1995.
2   It would be more precise to speak here of 'danger', since 'risk' denotes calculable insecurity, whereas (second order) 'danger' denotes incalculable insecurity (stemming from the characteristic choices of a civilization). See U. Beck, 'Überlebensfragen, Sozialstruktur und ökologische Aufklärung', in idem, *Politik in der Risikogesellschaft*, Frankfurt/Main 1991, pp. 117–40.
3   This is ultimately the tone of the report by the Bavarian-Saxon Commission for Issues of the Future, which precisely did not (as many think) reaffirm the optimistic credo of neoliberalism, but pointed and painted up its darker side. I owe a lot of information and ideas to my work in this commission, although the picture drawn in this book goes in a different direction.
4   André Gorz, *Arbeit zwischen Elend und Utopie*, Frankfurt/Main 1999.
5   Cf. David J. Elkins, *Beyond Sovereignty*, Toronto 1995, p. 7.
6   I am deeply grateful to Wolfgang Bonß, Ludger Preis and Peter Felixberger for important suggestions that helped me in reworking the text.
7   See the contributions by C. Meier and K. P. Liessmann in U. Beck (ed.), *Die Zukunft von Arbeit und Demokratie*, Frankfurt/Main 1999.
8   Meinhard Miegel, discussion contribution to Alfred-Herrhausen-Gesellschaft (ed.), *Arbeit der Zukunft, Zukunft der Arbeit*, Stuttgart 1994, p. 133.
9   M. Miegel, 'Sozialstaat Deutschland', in H. Glaser and R. Lindemann (eds), *Arbeit in der Krise – von der Notwendigkeit des Umdenkens*,

Cadolzburg 1998, pp. 141f. The 'job-killer' view of the world is much discussed in economic theory as a 'shake-out hypothesis' that appears from time to time (in the debate on machinery in the 1820s, the debate on automation in the 1960s, and so on). The only alternative presented to it is the 'compensatory hypothesis', according to which technological advances always create enough new possibilities of employment. See Bernhard Jahoda, 'Technologischer Fortschritt und Beschäftigung', in ibid.

10 André Gorz, *Abschied vom Proletariat*, Reinbek 1980; cf. the English edition, *Farewell to the Working Class*, London 1980, pp. 11–12.

11 See U. Beck, A. Giddens and S. Lash, *Reflexive Modernization: Politics, Tradition and Aesthetics in the Modern Social Order*, Cambridge 1994, pp. 175ff.

12 See Dietmar Brock, 'Wirtschaft und Staat im Zeitalter der Globalisierung', *Aus Politik und Zeitgeschichte*, 33–4/1997, p. 18.

13 Saskia Sassen, *The Global City*, Princeton 1991.

14 See Richard Gordon, *Internationalization, Multinationalization, Globalization*, Santa Cruz, 1994.

15 Elkins, *Beyond Sovereignty*, pp. 115f.

16 See the contributions by Maarten Hajer and Sven Kesselring to U. Beck et al. (eds), *Der unscharfe Ort der Politik*, Opladen 1999.

17 Mary Kaldor, 'Reconceptualizing Organized Violence', in Daniele Archibugi, David Held and Martin Köhler (eds), *Reimagining Political Community*, Cambridge 1998, pp. 91–110.

18 James N. Rosenau, 'Governance and Democracy in a Globalizing World', in Archibugi et al. (eds), *Reimagining Political Community*, p. 28.

19 See OECD, *Main Economic Indicators*, Paris 1995.

20 Peter F. Drucker, *Postcapitalist Society*, Oxford 1993, p. 7.

21 Figures taken from *Der Spiegel*, 1/1998.

22 C. Gauer and J. Scriba, *Die Standortlüge*, Frankfurt/Main 1998, p. 79.

23 See Jeremy Rifkin, *The End of Work: The Decline of the Global Labor Force and the Dawn of the Post-Market Era*, New York 1995.

24 Manuel Castells, *The Rise of the Network Society*, Oxford 1996, pp. 234, 475.

25 See U. Beck, *Gegengifte*, Frankfurt/Main 1988.

26 World Commission on Environment and Development, *Our Common Future*, London 1988, p. 8.

27 Ernst Ulrich von Weizsäcker, *Das Jahrhundert der Umwelt*, Frankfurt and New York 1999 – published by Campus Verlag in the same series as the German original of the present volume.

28 V. Shiva, 'Beijing Conference: Gender, Justice and Global Apartheid' (*Third World Resurgence* 61/62), in V. Aiithal (ed.), *Vielfalt als Stärke*.

Texte von Frauen aus dem Süden zur Vierten Weltkonferenz, Beijing 1995, p. 78.

29 See M. E. Porter, *The Competitive Advantage of Nations*, London 1990.

30 Thomas Westphal, 'Programmiertes Wachstum und moderner Kapitalismus', *Zeitschrift für sozialistische Politik und Wirtschaft* 4/1998, p. 27, which also contains the reference to Michael Porter. (See also H. Hern and M. Schumann, 'Kontinuität oder Pfadwechsel? Das deutsche Produktionsmodell am Scheideweg', in B. Cattero (ed.), *Modell Deutschland, Modell Europa*, Opladen 1998, pp. 85–98.) John Gray, for his part, makes two points in *False Dawn* that cast a somewhat different light on this pessimistic diagnosis of the 'social market economy' in Germany. First, no economy other than the West German one could have integrated a bankrupt state economy such as that of the GDR. Second, the 'Rhine model of capitalism', because of its position at the heart of a Europe of open frontiers, may precisely be the one that is built up and consolidated anew in a context of fundamental reforms.

31 Peter Fischer, *Die Selbstständigen von morgen*, Frankfurt/Main 1995, p. 40.

32 C. Clermont and J. Goebel, 'Muddling Through – Thesen zur Arbeitswelt von heute', manuscript, Berlin 1997.

33 *Newsweek*, 14 June 1993.

34 E. McLaughlin, *Flexibility in Work and Benefits*, London 1994; J. Millar, K. Cooke and E. McLaughlin, 'The Employment Lottery', *Policy and Politics* 17/1 (1989), pp. 75–81; Lawrence M. Mead and Frank Field, *From Welfare to Work*, London 1997.

35 Castells, *The Rise of the Network Society*, p. 476.

36 Peter Maiwald, 'Solidarität ist wie Mundgeruch', *Die Presse* ('Spektrum' section), 20–1 June 1998, p. iii. This scenario is developed further in chapter 5 on the 'risk regime'.

37 Elisabeth Beck-Gernsheim, *Männerwelt Beruf, Frauenwelt Familie*, Frankfurt/Main 1982.

38 See S. Greenhouse, 'Permanently Temporary', *International Herald Tribune*, 31 March 1998, p. 15.

39 Centre de Jeunes Dirigeants, Paris 1995, p. 125.

40 See Gorz, *Arbeit zwischen Elend und Utopie*.

41 F. Bergmann, 'New Work. Neue Arbeitsmodelle für die Zukunft', *Zukunft* 23, 1998, pp. 18f.

42 Friedrich Nietzsche, *The Gay Science* [1887], New York 1974, pp. 259–60.

43 See Christian Graf von Krockow, *Der deutsche Niedergang*, Stuttgart 1998, pp. 182ff; Bernd Guggenberger, 'Arbeit, Zeit und Muße', *Zukünfte* 23/1998, pp. 15ff.

44   See Willi Bierter and Uta von Winterfeld (eds), *Zukunft der Arbeit – welcher Arbeit?*, Wuppertal 1998.
45   Lars Clausen, *Produktive Arbeit, destruktive Arbeit*, Berlin and New York 1988.
46   The desperate search for jobs makes it tempting to forget the long history of critiques of wage-labour and hyper-specialization, from Karl Marx to Ivan Illich. See also Michael Brater and Ulrich Beck, *Berufliche Arbeitsteilung und soziale Ungleichheit*, Frankfurt/Main 1975, especially the chapter entitled 'A Critique of Special Trades and Occupations'.
47   See Michel Aglietta, *A Theory of Capitalist Regulation*, London 1979.
48   S. Willeke and T. Kleine-Brockhoff, 'Tut Modernisierung weh?', *Die Zeit*, 19 November 1998, p. 21.
49   W. Bonß, 'Zukunftsszenarien der Arbeit', in Beck, *Die Zukunft von Arbeit und Demokratie*.
50   On these dimensions, see also ibid.
51   Ibid., p. 34.
52   *Die Zeit*, 19 November 1998, p. 21.
53   All quotations are from Willeke and Kleine-Brockhoff, 'Tut Modernisierung weh?', in Beck (ed.), *Die Zukunft von Arbeit und Demokratie*.
54   M. Promberger et al., *Weniger Geld, kürzere Arbeitszeit, sichere Jobs?*, Berlin 1997; K. Jürgens and K. Reinecke, *Zwischen Volks- und Kinderwagen*, Berlin 1998.
55   R. Stadler, 'Die Saison-Professoren', *Süddeutsche Zeitung*, 20 October 1998, p. V 2/16.
56   Corinna Emundts, 'Fleiß zum Niedrigpreis', *Süddeutsche Zeitung*, 20 August 1998, p. 3.
57   Doris Metz, 'Existenzgründer – wie Tagelöhner gehalten', *Süddeutsche Zeitung*, 27 February 1998, p. 10.
58   *Süddeutsche Zeitung*, 7 April 1998, p. 2.
59   *Focus* 15, 1998, p. 28, quoted from Sylke Nissen, 'Neustrukturierung des Arbeitsmarktes', *Gewerkschaftliche Monatshefte* 6–7, 1998, p. 430.
60   OECD, *Employment Outlook*, Paris 1996, pp. 8 and 192.
61   'Permanently Temporary: High-Tech Firms Rely on Working Class', *International Herald Tribune*, 31 March 1998, pp. 1, 15.
62   P. G. Vobruba, 'Ende der Vollbeschäftigungsgesellschaft', *Zeitschrift für Sozialreform*, 1998, pp. 77f.
63   Ralf Dahrendorf, 'Neue Weltordnung', *DU – die Zeitschrift der Kultur*, vol. 5, May 1997, p. 17.
64   D. Schelsky and R. Zoller, 'Einleitung', in idem (eds), *Brasilien, Die Unordnung des Fortschritts*, Frankfurt/Main 1994, p. 7.

65 R. Zoller, 'Staat und Wirtschaftsentwicklung in Brasilien', in ibid., p. 360.

66 See also Ludger Pries, *Wege und Visionen von Erwerbsarbeit – Erwerbsverläufe und Arbeitsorientierungen abhängig und selbstständig Beschäftigter in Mexiko*, Frankfurt/Main 1997, p. 4. This section owes many of its ideas, arguments and empirical references to Pries's meticulous and factually rich study.

67 Ibid., p. 371.

68 Lais Abramo, 'The Sociology of Work in Latin America', *Work and Occupations*, 25/3, 1998, p. 306.

69 Jorge G. Castaneda, *The Mexican Shock: Its Meaning for the US*, New York 1995, p. 34.

70 Pries, *Wege und Visionen von Erwerbsarbeit*, p. 1.

71 Ibid., p. 109.

72 Ibid., p. 160.

73 Manuel Castells and Alejandro Portes, 'World Underneath: The Origins, Dynamics and Effects of the Informal Economy', in Portes et al. (eds), *The Informal Economy*, Baltimore 1989, p. 12.

74 Dahrendorf, p. 18.

75 'Das Manifest der glücklichen Arbeitslosen', in Beck (ed.), *Die Zukunft von Arbeit und Demokratie*.

76 Michael Lind, *The Next American Nation*, New York 1995, p. 216.

77 Silvio Zavalla (1998), quoted from Pries, *Wege und Visionen von Erwerbsarbeit*, p. 36.

78 See Christian Nürnberger, 'Freiheit macht arm', *Süddeutsche Zeitung*, 30 April–1 May 1998.

79 See Zygmunt Bauman, *Globalization*, Cambridge 1998, pp. 56ff.

80 M. Wolf, 'Veränderung von unten', in Schilsky and Zoller (eds), pp. 344f.

81 B. Barber, 'Räumen Sie doch mal auf! Gespräch über die Zukunft der Demokratie', *Die Zeit*, 29 October 1998, p. 58.

82 See Michael Walzer, 'Multiculturalism and Individualism', *Dissent*, Spring 1994, pp. 185–91.

83 'American Values', *The Economist*, 5 September 1992, cited from Berndt Ostendorf, 'The Politics of Difference: Theories and Practice in a Comparative US-German Perspective', lecture delivered at Georgetown University, March 1995, pp. 9f.

84 John Gray, *False Dawn*, London 1998, p. 104.

85 These figures are taken from the report of the Bavarian-Saxon Commission for Issues of the Future, vol. 1, Bonn 1996.

86 Gray, p. 113 – quoting Edward Luttwak, 'Turbo-Charged Capitalism and its Consequences', *London Review of Books*, 2 November 1995, p. 7.

87   See Robert D. Putnam, 'Symptome einer Krise – die USA, Europa und Japan im Vergleich', in Werner Weidenfeld (ed.), *Die Demokratie am Wendepunkt*, Munich 1997, pp. 52–80.

88   See T. Putnam, *Making Democracy Work*, Harvard 1995; and idem, 'Bowling Alone: America's Declining Social Capital', *Journal of Democracy*, vol. 6/1, pp. 65–78.

89   Robert D. Putnam, pp. 71f.

90   Ibid., p. 164.

91   Gray, p. 129.

92   Fresh confirmation of this has been provided by the Red-Green victory in the German elections of autumn 1998.

93   Shalini Randeria, 'Against the Self-Sufficiency of Western Social Sciences', unpublished manuscript, Berlin 1998.

94   C. Leadbeater, *The Rise of the Social Entrepreneur*, London 1997.

95   Ibid., pp. 30ff.

96   M. Köhler, 'From National to Cosmopolitan Public Sphere', in Archibugi et al., *Reimagining Political Community*, p. 232.

97   Ibid., p. 243.

98   M. Klingst, 'Die Mauerbauer', *Die Zeit*, 3 December 1998, p. 6.

99   P. Hassner, 'Refugees: A Special Case for Cosmopolitan Citizenship?', in Archibugi et al. (eds), *Reimagining Political Community*, p. 284.

100   D. Klages, 'Redebeitrag', in Bergedorfer Gesprächkreis (ed.), *Wachsende Ungleichheiten – neue Spaltungen? Exklusion als Gefahr für die Bürgergesellschaft*, Hamburg n.d., pp. 42, 86.

101   D. Buhl, 'Ungestylt und basisnah', *Die Zeit*, 2 December 1998, p. 4.

102   S. Franks, *Having None of It: Women, Men and the Future of Work*, London 1999, p. 6.

103   G. Notz, *Die neuen Freiwilligen*, AG Spak 1998. See also G. Salm, 'Bürgerarbeit ist keine Ersatzarbeit', *tageszeitung*, 3 November 1998.

104   J. Mitschke, 'Bürgergeld', *Volkswirtschaftliche Korrespondenz* 8/1995.

105   C. Pfeiffer, 'Gesprächsbeitrag', in Bergedorfer Gesprächskreis (ed.), p. 85.

106   M. Kempe, 'Ein Leben jenseits der Arbeitslosigkeit', *tageszeitung*, 19 October 1998, p. 12.

107   Ibid.

108   Buhl, p. 4.

109   Ronald Inglehart, *Modernization and Post-modernization – Cultural, Economic, and Political Change in 43 Societies*, Princeton 1997, pp. 78ff. Inglehart's work has given rise to a lively debate; see C. Beau and E. Papadakis, 'Polarised Priorities or Flexible Alternatives?', *International Journal of Public Opinion*, vol. 6/3, 1997.

185

110 H. Klages, 'Engagement und Engagementpotential in Deutschland', in Beck (ed.), *Die Zukunft von Arbeit und Demokratie*.

111 J. Mayrowitz, 'Die generalisierte Anderswo', in U. Beck (ed.), *Perspektiven der Weltgesellschaft*, p. 186.

112 Manuel Castells, *The Power of Identity*, Oxford 1997, esp. chs. 3 and 7.

113 Stefan Wray, in another book in the series of which the German edition of this volume is part (Florian Rötzer, *Megamaschine Wissen*), also speaks of the role of the Internet in this connection.

114 M. Toscano, *Turbulencia política*.

115 A. Appadurai, 'Globale ethnische Räume, Bemerkungen und Fragen zur Entwicklung einer transnationalen Anthropologie', in U. Beck (ed.), *Perspektiven der Weltgesellschaft*, p. 22.

116 W. Pierce, *National Vanguard*, quoted in Castells, *The Power of Identity*, p. 84.

117 K. Stern, 'A Force upon the Plain', quoted in Castells, *The Power of Identity*, pp. 84f.

118 See M. Albrow, *The Global Age: State and Society beyond Modernity*, Cambridge 1996.

119 For a detailed discussion of this, see Hartmut Graßl, *Wetterwende*, also published in the same series as the original German edition of this volume.

120 Anja Hof, 'Frauen-Netzwerke im Spannungsfeld von Globalisierung und Vielfalt', in Ruth Klingebiel and Shalini Randeria (eds), *Globalisierung aus Frauensicht*, Bonn 1998, p. 67.

121 Kumar-D'Fouza, 'The Universality of Human Rights Discourse', in Aruna Gnanadason et al. (World Council of Churches), *Women, Violence and Non-Violent Change*, Geneva 1996, p. 31; quoted (and retranslated) from Anja Hof, 'Frauen-Netzwerke'.

122 Martin Albrow, *Abschied vom Nationalstaat*, pp. 224f; cf. *The Global Age: State and Society beyond Modernity*, Cambridge 1996, upon which the German edition is based.

123 Anthony Giddens, *The Third Way: The Renewal of Social Democracy*, Cambridge 1998, p. 53.

124 See U. Beck, 'The Cosmopolitan Perspective: On the Sociology of the Second Age of Modernity', *British Journal of Sociology* (printing), 1999.

125 See Elisabeth Beck-Gernsheim, *Schwarze gibt es in allen Hautfarben*, Frankfurt/Main 1999.

126 I. Kant, 'Der ewige Frieden, Reflexion 8077', in *Handschriftlicher Nachlaß: Gesammelte Werke*, Frankfurt/Main 1969.

Select Bibliography

Aiithal, V. (ed.), *Vielfalt als Stärke. Texte von Frauen aus dem Süden zur Vierten Weltkonferenz*, Beijing 1995.

Albrow, M., *The Global Age: State and Society beyond Modernity*, Cambridge 1996.

Alfred-Herrhausen-Gesellschaft (ed.), *Arbeit der Zukunft, Zukunft der Arbeit*, Stuttgart 1994.

Archibugi, D., Held, D. and Köhler, M. (eds), *Reimagining Political Community*, Cambridge 1998.

Beck, U. (ed.), *Perspektiven der Weltgesellschaft*, Frankfurt/Main 1998.

Beck, U., 'The Cosmopolitan Perspective: On the Sociology of the Second Age of Modernity, *British Journal of Sociology*, vol. 51, no. 1, 2000.

Beck, U., *World Risk Society*, Cambridge 1999.

Beck, U. (ed.), *Die Zukunft von Arbeit und Demokratie*, Frankfurt/Main 1999.

Beck, U., *What is Globalization?*, Cambridge 2000.

Beck, U. et al. (eds), *Der unscharfe Ort der Politik*, Opladen 1999.

Beck, U., Giddens, A. and Lash, S. (eds), *Reflexive Modernization: Politics, Tradition and Aesthetics in the Modern Social Order*, Cambridge 1994.

Beck, U. and Beck-Gernsheim, E., *Individualization*, London (forthcoming).

Beck-Gernsheim, E., *Männerwelt Beruf, Frauenwelt Familie*, Frankfurt/Main 1982.

Beck-Gernsheim, E., *Juden, Deutsche und andere Mißverständnisse*, Frankfurt/Main 2000.

Bergedorfer Gesprächskreis (ed.), *Wachsende Ungleichheiten – neue Spaltungen? Exklusion als Gefahr für die Bürgergesellschaft*, Hamburg n.d.

Select Bibliography

Bierter, W. and Winterfeld, U. von (eds), *Zukunft der Arbeit – welcher Arbeit?*, Wuppertal 1998.

Bridges, W., *Jobshift: How to Prosper in a World without Jobs*, London 1995.

Castaneda, J., *The Mexican Shock: Its Meaning for the US*, New York 1995.

Castells, M., *The Rise of the Network Society*, Oxford 1996.

Castells, M., *The Power of Identity*, Oxford 1997.

Cattero, B. (ed.), *Modell Deutschland, Modell Europa*, Opladen 1998.

Clausen, L., *Produktive Arbeit, destruktive Arbeit*, Berlin and New York 1998.

Clermont, C. and Goebel, J., Muddling Through – Thesen zur Arbeitswelt von heute, manuscript, Berlin 1997.

Drucker, P. F., *Postcapitalist Society*, Oxford 1993.

Elkins, D. J., *Beyond Sovereignty*, Toronto 1995.

Fischer, P., *Die Selbstständigen von morgen*, Frankfurt/Main 1995.

Franks, S., *Having None of It: Women, Men and the Future of Work*, London 1999.

Gauer, C. and Scriba, J., *Die Standortlüge*, Frankfurt/Main 1998.

Giddens, A., *The Third Way: The Renewal of Social Democracy*, Cambridge 1998.

Glaser, H. and Lindemann, R. (eds), *Arbeit in der Krise – von der Notwendigkeit des Umdenkens*, Cadolzburg 1998.

Gnanadason, A. et al. (World Council of Churches), *Women, Violence and Non-Violent Change*, Geneva 1996.

Gordon, R., *Internationalization, Multinationalization, Globalization*, Santa Cruz 1994.

Gorz, A., *Arbeit zwischen Elend und Utopie*, Frankfurt/Main 1999.

Gorz, A., *Farewell to the Working Class*, London 1982.

Hassner, P., 'Refugees: A Special Case for Cosmopolitan Citizenship', in Archibugi et al. (1998).

Hauff, V. (ed.), *Unsere gemeinsame Zukunft*, Greven 1987.

Held, D., McGrew, H., Goldblatt, D. and Perration J., *Global Transformations*, Cambridge 1999.

Inglehart, R., *Modernization and Post-Modernization – Cultural, Economic, and Political Change in 43 Societies*, Princeton 1997.

International Labour Organization (ILO), *Laboral overview*, vol. 1 (1994), vol. 2 (1995), vol. 3 (1996), Lima (Regional Office for Latin America and the Caribbean).

Jürgens, K. and Reinecke, K., *Zwischen Volks- und Kinderwagen*, Berlin 1998.

Klingebiel, R. and Randeria, S. (eds), *Globalisierung aus Frauensicht*, Bonn 1998.

Kommission für Zukunftsfragen der Freistaaten Bayern und Sachsen, *Bericht*, Band I, Bonn 1996.

Krockow, C. Graf von, *Der deutsche Niedergang*, Stuttgart 1998.

Leadbeater, C., *The Rise of the Social Entrepreneur*, London 1997.

Select Bibliography

Lind, M., *The Next American Nation*, New York 1995.

McLaughlin, E., *Flexibility in Work and Benefits*, London 1994.

Mead, L. and Field, F., *From Welfare to Work*, London 1997.

Nietzsche, F., *The Gay Science* [1887], translated by Walter Kaufmann, New York 1974.

OECD, *Main Economic Indicators*, Paris 1995.

OECD, *Employment Outlook*, Paris 1996.

Porter, M. E., *The Competitive Advantage of Nations*, London 1990.

Pries, L., *Wege und Visionen von Erwerbsarbeit – Erwerbsverläufe und Arbeitsorientierungen abhängig und selbständig Beschäftigter in Mexiko*, Frankfurt/Main 1997.

Promberger, M. et al., *Weniger Geld, kürzere Arbeitszeit, sichere Jobs?*, Berlin 1997.

Putnam, T., *Making Democracy Work*, Harvard 1995.

Rifkin, J., *The End of Work: The Decline of the Global Labor Force and the Dawn of the Post-Market Era*, New York 1995.

Sassen, S., *The Global City*, Princeton 1991.

Schelsky, D. and Zoller, R. (eds), *Brasilien. Die Unordnung des Fortschritts*, Frankfurt/Main 1994.

Sennett, R., *The Corrosion of Character: The Personal Consequences of Work in the New Capitalism*, New York 1998.

Weidenfeld, W. (ed.), *Die Demokratie am Wendepunkt*, Munich 1997.

Index

Page references in italic indicate figures and tables

Index

Index

Index

Index

Index

Index

Index

198

Index

Index

Index

structural 43
United States
  and Brazilianization 104, 110–20
  and civil labour 139, 145
  compared with Germany 111–12, 113
  and crime and punishment 116–18
  and critique of Chicago School 118–20
  and decay of social capital 115–16
  and erosion of middle class 114
  and ethnicity as class 116–18
  and female employment 39
  and Fordism 69, 118
  and freedom and equality 110–12
  and informalization of work 110–11, 115
  and job insecurity 113–14, 118
  'jobs miracle' 1, 43, 44, 91, 102, 112, 115–16
  and labour market deregulation 82–3, 117
  and labour market flexibility 59, 85, 110
  and neoliberalism 56, 112, 119
  and political action 115–16
  and social exclusion 107–9, 119
  and technology and work 39, 43
  and unemployment and poverty 2, 44–5, 111, 117
  and university jobs 82–3
  work and democracy in 110–20
Urry, John 22, 40
utopianism, free-market 1, 4, 5, 112, 114, 119

violence, xenophobic 52, 135–6
virtuality, virtual companies 73, 85
Vobruba, P. G. 90
Volkswagen, labour policies 79–80, 81

wages
  increase 69
  reduction 45, 67, 81
  'shadow' 142
Wallerstein, Immanuel 74
Walzer, Michael 111
Weber, Max 24
Weizsäcker, Ernst Ulrich von 49
welfare, 'active' 154–5
welfare state
  and active citizens 6
  and capitalism 4, 17
  and dependency 96–7
  and first modernity 17–18
  and individualization 53
  and second modernity 21
  threats to 3, 4, 51
  and work 102
Western, Bruce 116
Westphal, Thomas (quoted) 52
Willeke, and Kleine-Brockhoff, (quoted) 79–80
Wolf, M. (quoted) 107–8
women
  and civic labour 6, 142–3
  in employment 39, 51, 61, 64, 88, 142–3; and breaks 7; job insecurity 93; part-time 7, 50, 56, 60, 94; working time 81
  and family labour 6, 160
  and multi-activity 2, 6, 92
  and transnational networks 166–7
work
  and capitalism without work 37, 38 42–4
  and civil labour 15, 60, 142, 145–9
  despatialization 41, 73
  ecologization 48–50
  feminization 64
  and free-time society 5–6, 7, 37, 58, 61–2, 65
  and freedom 11

201

Index

Index compiled by Meg Davies